130 WAYS TO INVOLVE PARENTS

IN YOUTH MINISTRY

Group
Loveland, Colorado

130 Ways to Involve Parents in Youth Ministry
Copyright © 1994 Group Publishing, Inc.

Credits
Compiled and edited by Martin Nagy
Cover designed by Liz Howe
Cover illustration by Joel Armstrong
Interior designed by Lisa Smith

Contributors
David Adams, Dub Ambrose, Barbara Beach, Paul Borthwick, Brent Bromstrup, Drew Crislip, Karen Dockrey, Mike Gillespie, Jon Hathorn, Thomas Hoehner, Dr. Larry Keefauver, Rick Lawrence, Walt Marcum, David Messer, Joseph Moore, Margie Morris, Walt Mueller, Barbie Murphy, Martin Nagy, Mike Nappa, Stephen Parolini, Roy Crowe, David Shaheen, Nancy Shaw, Marjorie Sims, Kristine Tomasik, Bodie Weiss, Christine Yount

Scriptures quoted from The Youth Bible, New Century Version, copyright © 1991 by Word Publishing, Dallas, Texas 75039. Used by permission.

Library of Congress Cataloging-in-Publication Data
130 ways to involve parents in youth ministry.
     p.   cm.
  ISBN 1-55945-250-1
  1. Church work with teenagers. 2. Parent and teenager. I. Group Publishing. II. Title: One hundred thirty ways to involve parents in youth ministry. III. Title: One hundred and thirty ways to involve parents in youth ministry. IV. Title: Hundred thirty ways to involve parents in youth ministry.
BV4447.A16 1994
259'.23'085—dc20   94-23152
                                                  CIP

10 9 8 7 6 5 4 3 2   03 02 01 00 99 98 97 96 95
Printed in the United States of America.

CONTENTS

INTRODUCTION

Here's a riddle for you:

How do you create a vibrant youth ministry, tailored to your kids' needs, using skills and resources you may not have, without burning yourself out in the process?

What's the answer? *Parents.*

Few people would argue with the value of involving parents in youth ministry. After all, parents have hands-on, day-to-day experience working with kids. And parents offer a diverse resource of skills and abilities. But most youth workers would agree that it can be a struggle to get parents involved.

Here's another riddle for you:

Where can you find over 100 innovative ideas to help parents play a vital role in your youth group?

The answer is in your hands: *130 Ways to Involve Parents in Youth Ministry.*

In this book you'll find:

● ideas for making parents your partners in ministry;

● tips for coordinating successful parent meetings and support groups;

● activities that give parents and kids opportunities to grow together, have fun together, communicate, and serve together;

● creative ways to encourage and inform parents;

● strategies for handling conflict with parents; and

● photocopiable fast forms to make involving parents in your ministry quick and easy.

Now that you've opened the book, start thumbing through it. Think about how you might tailor these ideas to fit your own youth group's needs. Then use *130 Ways to Involve Parents in Youth Ministry* to build a deeper, stronger, fuller youth ministry that's good for your kids, their parents, and you.

PART 1

PARENTS
as Partners

JOBS FOR PARENTS

If we approached fishing the way we often approach recruiting parents, we'd probably drive to the river's edge, honk the car horn, then pray for the fish to leap into the ice chest on the back seat. This kind of recruiting is better labeled "wishful thinking." Hoping and honking just don't work.

You'll "catch" more parents when you use creative approaches for involving parents. Here's a tackle box full of ideas that'll hook parents into your ministry and help make your ministry more efficient and effective.

▼ ▼ ▼ ▼ ▼ ▼ ▼ ▼ ▼ ▼ ▼ ▼ ▼ ▼ ▼ ▼ ▼ ▼ ▼ ▼

Administrative Assistance

At times, the pressures of paperwork can make youth ministry seem like mostly typing, copying, and filling out forms. Why not recruit parents to take over some administrative duties? For example:

● If you're stuck pecking out meeting plans or letters on your computer, ask a parent to volunteer a couple of hours each week to do inputting for you;

● If your church can't afford a secretary for you, ask an available parent to "tithe" some time to your ministry by doing paperwork for you; or

● If you need letters, fliers, articles, or handouts photocopied to keep parents and kids informed, ask an available parent to make copies, collate pages, and, when necessary, call publishers for permission to photocopy resources.

Using parents as administrative assistants gives them a valuable role to play *and* frees you up to do your job better—helping their kids grow in their relationships with God.

Bulletin Board Caretakers

Recruit parents to maintain a bulletin board with news of upcoming events, pictures, accolades, affirmations, and thank-you notes. Kids will soon grow accustomed to checking on the bulletin board to see what's new, and both parents and teenagers will have an easy source of information about your youth group.

Calligraphers and Artists

Creative printing or artwork adds a valuable touch to your regular youth group publications. When you're tired of using clip art, recruit parents who are skilled calligraphers or artists and put them to work on your invitations, announcements, and posters.

Camp Counselors

Involve parents as summer camp counselors. Since many parents will have to ask for time off work, be sure to get a commitment well in advance of the camp.

Hold a meeting to discuss the responsibilities parents might have as camp counselors, such as leading a devotion, worship time, or nature hike. Assign roles based on parents' interests and abilities so parents know what to expect, and they can enjoy the camp more. At this meeting, give parents a packet of resources they can use to prepare for the camp. In the packet include things such as a camp schedule, directions to and from the camp, a bibliography of resources to read before the camp, tips for relating to kids in a camp setting, guidelines for disciplinary situations, important phone numbers, and so on.

Then, at the camp, turn parents loose to do what they do best. Make yourself available as a resource to parents, answering questions and gathering supplies as needed.

Child-Care Providers for Volunteer Youth Workers

At times it's hard for youth ministry volunteers who are also parents of young children to find child-care providers during youth functions. One good source of child care for the children of your volunteer workers is other parents. Youth group parents appreciate the work other people do with their teenagers and are often happy to return the favor by baby-sitting young children during youth meetings or events.

Poll parents to see who is willing to help out your ministry in this way. Then put together a pool of parents who will provide child care for your leaders. Rotate child-care responsibilities with the other parents in the pool. If possible, find a room on the church grounds for child care. Give parents who can't make a regular commitment the option to act as substitutes for those in the child-care pool.

As with any child-care venture, screen adults carefully, choosing only the most responsible and trustworthy people to care for your volunteer youth workers' children.

Clown Ministers

Survey parents' talents—you may find an experienced (or simply willing) clown or two in your midst. Invite clowns to create a comic routine and present it during a youth meeting. Or have a clown take a regular part of your meetings, such as making announcements or leading games. You might also give clowns a segment of a retreat.

If you or your kids' parents are interested in starting a clown ministry, but aren't sure how to go about it, check out *Clown Ministry* by Floyd Shaffer and Penne Sewall, and *Clown Ministry Skits for All Seasons* by Floyd Shaffer. Both of these creative resources are available from Group Publishing.

Coaches

Many parents coach local sports teams. Ask if they'd be willing to coach a church team if you started one.

Talk to parents with skills in basketball, volleyball, softball, soccer, or other sports your kids are interested in. Then see about getting a team from your youth group involved in a city or church league in your area.

Or start a new sports league with other churches in your community. Recruit a parent with good organizational skills to be a "league commissioner" who works with you to recruit teams, set league policy, secure facilities, and balance the league budget. Call your local community center or high school sports association to find out about hiring referees and officials.

Discipleship and Sharing Group Participants

A discipleship and sharing group gives kids a safe place to defuse their emotions and struggle to make sense of the conflicting perspectives, behaviors, attitudes, fears, and joys that life brings. This kind of group helps kids develop the tools they need to make decisions based on biblical principles.

A discipleship and sharing group is also an excellent place to get parents involved in youth ministry. Recruit parents to lead discipleship and sharing groups or to simply act as a fellow group member who brings a parental viewpoint to the discussion.

Express to parents the importance of a sharing group and the commitment involved. Explain that kids are allowing themselves to be vulnerable, exploring issues in a open, non-threatening, and interactive forum. Parent participants need to have a strong commitment to the sharing group and the kids. Ask leaders to commit to being a part of the group for at least one school year.

Assign kids to sharing groups randomly or by gender or age. If you use gender assignments, have a male adult lead the guys' group and a female lead the girls. If you have age assignments, have parents with children in the higher grades participate in groups with younger kids. For example, have the parents of a senior lead a group of sophomores. That way, parents can draw from their own kids' experiences to help their discipleship-group members.

Developing rapport between parent participants and teenagers is important to the success of the group. But don't assume that a parent is ready to lead a sharing group just because kids are drawn to him or her. Ask parents what kind of training they want and need, then do your best to provide that training through seminars, workshops, books, one-on-one interviews with experts, and so on.

Give group leaders a video from the *Hot Talk-Starter Video Series* or a copy of the book *Controversial Discussion Starters* by Stephen Parolini to help groups examine current issues from a biblical perspective. Both of these resources are available from Group Publishing.

Drivers

Minivans are hot sellers these days, and you probably know several parents who own them. Ask those parents if they'd be willing to transport kids to youth group events occasionally.

Set up a schedule for the drivers so they'll know when they're needed. Have parents sign a commitment statement that lists the dates and times they're needed. Make sure everyone has a schedule and call parents a week before they're scheduled to drive to remind them of the time, date, and destination.

Experts and Speakers

Use parents as speakers and panel participants when discussing careers, college options, or the problems teenagers may have getting along with family members.

Invite parents who are involved in unique community programs such as D.A.R.E. or teenage pregnancy centers. Ask them to share the program's purpose and why they got involved.

To make sure parents focus on information kids are interested in, have your teenagers prepare anonymous questions on 3×5 cards in advance. Then give the guest parent(s) copies of those cards and ask him or her to answer the most pressing questions during the presentation. Have speakers plan for a time of spontaneous questions from the youth group members at the meeting.

Family-Picnic Organizers

Ask a small committee of parents to organize an afternoon picnic that includes fun as well as serious family interaction. (See the "Adventures and Activities for Parents and Teenagers" section beginning on page 36 for a wide variety of ideas that can be adapted for use during a family picnic.)

Have parents on the committee divide the key responsibilities for the picnic. For example, have different parents choose and secure the picnic site, publicize the event, determine the menu, and acquire the food (such as through a sign-up list or having everyone bring their own), coordinate any activities or entertainment during the picnic, and so on.

A family picnic can be an event unto itself, lay the groundwork for a family retreat, or make a fun reunion after a retreat.

Fun-and-Games Family-Night Participants

Recruit a few parents to plan an annual "Fun-and-Games Family Night" for your youth group. Invite teenagers from your group to join with those parents to plan and lead the evening's recreation.

Tell parents and teenage planners that the sole purpose of the evening is nonstop fun for the families represented in the youth group and to plan accordingly. Have planners poll both parents and youth group members to find out what their favorite games, snacks, and entertainment are. Then choose the best ideas for inclusion in the event.

In addition, parents and teenage planners can create entirely new games or use ideas from the "Adventures and Activities for Parents and Teenagers" section beginning on page 36. Other great resources are *Great Group Games for Youth Ministry, Quick Crowdbreakers and Games for Youth Groups,* and *Have-A-Blast Games,* all available from Group Publishing.

Ask different parents to be on the planning committee each year so you get a wide variety of involvement and ideas at each new "Fun-and-Games Family Night." You might even consider holding this event more than once a year.

Fund-Raisers

Constantly having to raise funds for your youth group can be a draining and time-consuming task that diverts you from the main focus of your ministry—kids. Why not enlist parents to help?

Recruit a core of parents whose primary responsibility is to plan and coordinate all fund-raisers for your group. Let parents know which events need funding, how much money is needed, and who's in charge of planning the events.

Then turn loose your fund-raising parents to create and schedule fund-raiser programs and events throughout the year. Periodically, have parents from this core group report on their progress. Parents can also use this time to inform kids of the next fund-raising event and how kids can be involved.

Hosts for Home Parties

Some parents enjoy occasionally hosting get-togethers for the youth group in their homes. This allows parents to meet kids on the parents' turf and provides a way for kids to gain a new appreciation for parents. Ask for parent volunteers to open their homes. Offer one of the following options (or others of your own choosing) for get-together ideas.

● Give parents a schedule of school functions, sporting events, and youth ministry happenings. Then have parents sign up to host informal gatherings (afterglows) after several of the events. Ask the host parents (or other parents) to provide refreshments and a warm atmosphere for conversation and relaxation. If you have a food budget, give parents money to get snacks for the kids.

● Check around for parents whose homes lend themselves to youth group parties. For example, parents who either own or have access to swimming pools could host swim parties. Parents with large yards could host volleyball or Frisbee parties. Parents with large-screen televisions could host video parties. And parents with a cozy area in their homes could host "hot-cocoa-in-front-of-a-fireplace-while-you-study-for-finals" parties.

Lay Counselors for Teenagers

As a youth leader you're faced with counseling needs that, at times, can exceed your available time or expertise. Using parents to help counsel teenagers in crisis is both a practical and valuable way to help your kids get the care they need in times of trouble.

First, survey parents of your teenagers to find people with counseling or health-care backgrounds. Seek people who are qualified to lead a lay counseling program. Ask for professional references and a short résumé from each parent you are considering.

Next, ask qualified parents to create and head a lay counseling program for teenagers in which parent-counselors make time available to talk to kids on an individual basis about the problems they're facing. Contact a school counselor for advice and resources about a lay counseling program.

Ask your counseling program leaders to develop a standard counseling training program for all lay counselors to go through before actually meeting with kids. As part of your training program, have parents learn about available counseling resources and gain practical experience by sitting in on several counseling sessions with an experienced counselor.

Also, train counselors about what is (and isn't) appropriate for a nonprofessional counselor to handle. Two excellent resources for parents who are lay counselors are *Counseling Helpsheets* by Tom Klaus and G. Lamar Roth and *Counseling Teenagers* by Dr. G. Keith Olson. Both of these books are available from Group Publishing.

Local Advocates for Teenagers

Parents have a vested interest in the laws that affect their children, so use parents of teenagers in your youth group as advocates for young people. Encourage parents to act as local reporters and lobbyists to help your church stay informed and to get involved in issues that affect teenagers. Here are several ways to be effective advocates for teenagers.

● Have parents get to know your local, state, and national elected representatives by name *and* by their positions on issues that impact youth. Have advocates periodically poll your youth group kids to find out what issues concern them. Encourage advocates to look for newspaper articles concerning teenage issues and periodically ask your region's legislative services office what statutes affecting teenagers have recently been proposed or passed. Have advocates also ask an elected official's staff to respond to questions about their boss's views on teenage issues. Once a month or once a quarter, have your teenage advocates present the information they've gathered in the church bulletin or make presentations at parents and youth meetings.

● Have your teenage advocates write notes of encouragement when they agree with a local representative's views. Or have parents send a firm, yet courteous, letter outlining their views when they disagree with a lawmaker's stand. Letters should always be neat and concise and stick to one issue per contact.

When a key bill has just been introduced, it's important for advocates to correspond with local representatives. Remind parents to make follow-up contacts. A thank-you card when a lawmaker responds favorably to your advocates' input speaks volumes.

Have parents ask your representative to sponsor an appropriate youth-friendly law. Gather pertinent statistics, news clippings, even a similar law from another jurisdiction to bolster your case. Some legislators may even be willing to meet with your advocates or teenagers in your group to discuss their ideas and concerns.

● Encourage parents who prefer speaking over writing to ask for an appointment with an official. Elected officials will likely have just a few minutes to talk, so encourage parents to carefully prepare ahead of time what they want to say. If you have national concerns, encourage parents to call Capitol Hill Switchboard, (202) 224-3121 and ask for your U.S. representative or senator. Or they may call the White House Comments Office, (202) 456-1111.

Many ministries offer lobbying tips and issue-oriented resources. Three such ministries are the Family Research Council, 700 13th St. N.W., Ste. 500, Washington, D.C. 20005, (202) 393-2100; Christian Legal Fellowship, 100 Fullerton St., London, Ontario N6A 1K1, (519) 434-2803; and Concerned Women for America, Box 65453, Washington, D.C. 20035, (202) 488-7000.

Mimes

Adults with theater backgrounds may be eager to organize a mime troupe for special events, announcements, and retreats. Ask parent volunteers to train kids who are interested in mime and possibly start a mime ministry at your church.

Have parent and teenage mimes perform at nursing homes, children's homes, and hospitals. Or have them mime Scripture passages or inspirational stories at Sunday services, youth group meetings, or retreats.

Movement Leaders and Interpretive Dancers

Survey parents to find out if any of them are trained dancers. If it's appropriate within your church or denomination, find creative ways to incorporate their talents into your program.

For example, these parents could do an interpretive dance to a song, story, or Scripture passage geared toward teenagers at a youth group meeting or retreat. Ask dancers to teach kids simple dances to present during youth group worship time or at a congregational Sunday service. If possible, include a variety of dance styles ranging from ballet to modern.

Seek parents who are skilled in dance to sponsor and lead a youth group dance troupe. Through this troupe, they could teach interested kids the basics of dance and schedule opportunities for the troupe to perform.

Music Leaders

Look for gifted musicians, singers, and worship leaders among your parents. Have these parents lead music and worship at youth group meetings, events, and services.

Seek interested parents to form a small orchestra, band, or vocal ensemble to perform occasionally for your youth group or for a congregational service. If any youth group members are musicians, have them practice with the parents and help lead worship or perform as well.

Painters, Carpenters, Photographers, and More

Form a list of parents' occupations, then ask parents to help out when you've got a project that could benefit from their skills.

For example, ask parents who are painters or carpenters to help give your meeting room a facelift. Ask parents who are photographers to take pictures at a retreat. An accountant could keep track of your youth ministry budget, and a mechanic could service the youth group van. Have a firefighter discuss fire safety and a police officer explain local laws that affect teenagers, such as curfew or cruising laws.

Parent Advisory Board Members

A parent advisory board serves as a sounding board for the youth minister. It's a "think tank" on youth ministry within the church. It's an excellent way to involve parents and to ensure your program has a broad base of support.

Enlist about four to seven parents for your board. Then set up monthly meetings with them to discuss your church's youth ministry. Use these meetings to explore long-range goals, brainstorm ideas for the youth group, discuss the feasibility of new ideas, and evaluate the progress of ideas that are already being implemented.

If it's appropriate, invite youth group members to join a parent advisory board meeting from time to time. Publish a summary of your meetings in the church or youth group newsletter.

Parent Bible Study Leaders

Parents need spiritual nurturing as much as their kids do. So, recruit qualified parents to lead one or more parent Bible studies.

Ask parents who have experience in Bible study to plan and lead a special study for other parents. Schedule the parent Bible studies during the same time your youth group meets. Make Bible commentaries and adult curriculum (such as Group's *Apply-It-to-Life™ Adult Bible Series*) available to Bible study leaders. It might also be fun for parents to use the same curriculum the youth group does.

Let parents choose their own topics for the Bible studies or have them tie into the themes of their kids' youth meetings. Or, have Bible studies for specific groups such as dads, moms, single parents, or parents of blended families.

Parent Booster Club Members

Form a youth group booster club that's similar to a school, band, or athletic booster club. This is not a policy-setting group but a group that agrees to help out and encourage your teenagers when needed.

For example, boosters can help with fund raising and organizing, coordinate ideas for encouraging youth group members, or sponsor a "pep rally" for the kids in your group.

To assist booster club parents in their task, give them frequent updates about what's happening with the kids in the youth group, along with schedules of planned programs and events.

Parent Representatives on Church Committees

Incorrect or false information can damage a youth program, so encourage teenagers' parents to volunteer for church committees. If parents are well-informed and have input into the various church committees, they can make sure that what's said in these committees about the youth group is accurate. They can also be advocates for the youth program in areas such as finance or church space.

Give committee members regular updates about the youth group and quickly answer any questions they bring back from their committees. Call them regularly and get together for breakfast or lunch meetings to keep these parents informed.

Parent-Teenager Retreat Coordinators

Hold annual parent-teenager retreats for the families represented in your youth group. Focused programming at retreats can get families working and playing together, promote family communication, and encourage praying together and growing spiritually.

Ask a few parents to plan and coordinate the retreat for you. Encourage them to recruit other volunteers to help.

Parent coordinators and their volunteers can arrange entertainment, book speakers, plan activities, and gather supplies.

They can also find a place for the retreat, plan meals, buy food, and find cooks and servers. If participants need to pay for the retreat, have coordinators find people to collect and distribute the money appropriately. Have other coordinators publicize the retreat and lead the sessions.

To make sure everything is moving in an appropriate direction, check on coordinators' progress now and then, offering related resources as needed.

Parenting-Skills Teachers

As a ministry both to parents and to teenagers preparing for adulthood, ask adults who have parenting skills you respect to teach portions of a parenting class.

Classes can include caring for an infant, parenting small children, discipline issues, youth culture and issues, and family communication. Set up role-plays where parents get to walk in their kids' shoes and vice versa. See the "Meetings for Parents and Teenagers" section beginning on page 55 for ideas.

Or, conduct classes for parents of teenagers preparing to enter the youth group. Eight sessions could involve watching the *Parenting Teenagers Video Training Series* available from Group Publishing.

Parents Job-Description Committee

Parents don't want to jump into new responsibilities without knowing what they're getting into. Do your parents and your youth ministry both a favor by preparing job descriptions for parent volunteers.

First, recruit three or four parents to serve on a job-description committee. Then, together with these parents, create job descriptions for parent volunteers in your youth ministry. These job descriptions will help parents who volunteer be comforted by your organized and professional approach to ministry, and parents will be more likely to consider your invitation when you ask them to volunteer. Parents will also appreciate that other parents were involved in creating the job descriptions, thus making sure their interests were represented in the process.

Here are several things for your committee to consider when preparing a job description.

● Evaluate what *you* need and want and what *parents* need and want from a role in your youth ministry. Include this information in the job description.

● Determine your youth ministry goals and decide what skills you need to meet those goals. For example: If a goal is for each of the kids to feel like he or she can relate comfortably with at least one adult at youth group meetings, plan an equal mix of parent volunteers of both sexes and one adult for every four kids. Also, select parents who are good listeners, feel at home around kids, can commit to attend meetings regularly, and are secure in their faith. Communicate these expectations to parents through the job description.

● Create several job descriptions for parents to choose from, such as food coordinator, discussion leader, worship coordinator, events planner, newsletter editor, and so on. Let parents choose their top two or three job interests so you'll know which tasks they would enjoy.

● Be sure to make every task meaningful. Think through the tasks needed and explain how each task contributes in a meaningful way to your ministry. Parents who offer help and then are asked to do tasks that are perceived as mundane, "no-brainer" jobs will soon feel unneeded or unappreciated.

● In each job description, outline practical commitments expected from parent volunteers. For example, tell how much time parents can expect to put into a job each week or month, the tasks and responsibilities the job requires, how long a commitment is needed for this task (such as one month, six months, one year, or longer), the level of accountability necessary, expectations in regard to conduct, a schedule of required meetings, and a schedule of periodic time off.

● Provide a blank section on each job description for parents to identify the kind of training they need. For example, a parent may be interested in leading a discussion group, but might need training in small group dynamics. Try to provide any reasonable training requested by parents.

● Communicate enthusiasm for your ministry in the job descriptions. Point out the rewards of serving in youth ministry. Include a few quotes from kids in your group. Avoid making your youth ministry sound boring, too tough, or unworthy. Remember, you're offering parents an opportunity to impact lives for eternity. If you aren't excited about the job opportunities you're offering, no one else will be either.

Parents Newsletter Publishers

Parents appreciate being informed about your youth ministry. So why not let them take responsibility for informing each other? Put parents in charge of creating and publishing a parents newsletter.

For example, one church sends out a monthly parents newsletter titled "NETMA News." The acronym stands for "Nobody Ever Tells Me Anything." The NETMA News is written by parents and contains information of concern to parents.

The newsletter could simply include the dates, times, places, contact people, and other details for upcoming events and trips. Or, it could also include articles about youth group members and reports on youth events, camps, and trips. It could even be expanded to include parenting tips, youth trends, or a regular letter from the youth minister or pastor.

Parents Prayer Club

Recruit a group of parents who'll commit to praying regularly for your youth group. Arrange for them to meet on a weekly basis to pray for your kids, your leaders, and you. A prayer club could meet during a Sunday school hour, before or after church, or one evening during the week.

Label a box "Prayer Requests," and put it in your youth room with paper and pencils close by. Encourage kids and youth ministry leaders to write each prayer request on a slip of paper and put it in the box. Have "pray-ers" collect these slips prior to each prayer club meeting. The prayer club can also organize prayer chains for special circumstances and emergencies.

Part-Time Parents

For a variety of reasons, there are times when kids need more parenting attention than their own families can provide. Perhaps both parents work full time. More and more kids live in single-parent families. And many teenagers don't have adult role models in their lives.

Recruiting parents with time to share can enrich the lives of teenagers and adults alike. Ask these volunteer parents to play a "part-time parent" role for specific members of your youth group.

Remember: Communicate to part-time parents the importance of being sensitive to a teenager's real parents' feelings and plans. Make sure part-time parents understand that under no circumstance are they to try to replace a real parent's role in a teenager's life. Rather, a part-time parent should complement the real parents, supporting the family as a whole in his or her ministry to a teenager. For this to work, it's extremely important that the real parents are in favor of this setup from the outset. Gain approval and support from the real parents before pursuing people to act as part-time parents to their teenagers.

Part-time parents could invite "adopted" youth group members to join in family activities such as going to a movie or fishing. Part-time parents could also play big brother or big sister roles to teenagers in the youth group, plan one-on-one activities with teenagers from other families, offer to help teenagers with homework or school projects, attend school functions that a teenager's real parents can't attend, and so on.

Puppet Ministers

Puppets aren't just for children anymore. Teenagers can also be entertained and challenged by a skillful puppeteer or ventriloquist. Even parents who have never done puppet ministry can, with practice, quickly learn how to skillfully use a puppet.

If you have parents interested in a puppet ministry, give them *Puppets: Ministry Magic* by Dale and Liz VonSeggen as a resource for starting out (available from Group Publishing).

Then begin incorporating puppets into your meetings. Use puppets to give announcements, emcee events, direct games, or perform skits. For extra fun, encourage parents to involve teenagers in using the puppets.

Secret Encouragers

Recruit a group of parents to act as secret encouragers for your kids. Give each parent a portion of the names on your youth group roll and have them spend six months anonymously affirming their assigned kids.

Have parents send encouraging notes, leave small surprise gifts at youth meetings, or send balloons on kids' birthdays. At the end of the six months, have an "encouragers-revealed" party where kids meet their secret encouragers and express their appreciation.

Appoint someone to make sure that each teenager is being affirmed on a regular basis so none of your kids feel like they've been forgotten. Have this same person assign the secret encouragers and periodically check in with encouragers and kids to find out what kinds of things have been done and when.

Snacks and Meals

Food is always a winner among teenagers, but it can be tough to provide snacks on the average youth ministry budget. Here's where parents can help.

Ask group members' parents to take turns preparing and serving a snack (or even a meal!) as needed at group meetings and events. If parents rotate this service, they probably won't have to serve food more than two or three times a year. And you won't have to charge kids for their snacks or meals.

Sunday School Teachers

Parents have a built-in interest in what their kids hear at church. Capitalize on parents' convictions and put them to work as teachers in your Sunday school program. Try the following ideas:

● To avoid burnout, assign teaching teams in which parents work with one or more other parents to plan or teach the lessons. Three or four parents working together can divide the work. A team of teachers can also control a class better than one person.

● Have teachers recruit other parents to be their substitutes. Set up a buddy system so each parent-teacher has another parent who can serve as a substitute when requested. Some teachers may want to ask parents they already know. Have teachers call their substitutes when they need someone to fill in. This system will improve the success of finding replacements, as well as increase substitutes' sense of commitment.

● Involve parents when you're choosing your Sunday school curriculum. Bring three or four different curriculum options to a meeting and have parents look through them. Then solicit parents' opinions to help you decide which curriculum to use. This will help parents take ownership in the material they'll be teaching.

Supply Purchasers

When you need to buy supplies to use in your ministry, such as game supplies, food for events, and so on, give a parent (or two) your shopping list and ask him or her to do your purchasing for you.

Be sure to give shoppers your church's tax exempt numbers and make arrangements for the shopping to be done in time to meet your youth group's needs. If you receive special discounts at any stores, inform the shoppers about them.

This is good task for parents who feel more comfortable on the fringes of your ministry, and it frees your time for other things.

Telephone Callers

One of the easiest ways to include parents in your youth ministry is to have them do some phone calling for you. This frees up your time and helps parents get to know each other and the kids in the youth group. Try these ideas:

● On a rotating basis, ask different parents to make phone calls for event registration, event sign up, last-minute changes in plans, and so on.

● Set up a telephone chain. Put all the parents' names and phone numbers, as well as your own, on a master list. Give every parent a copy of the list. When you have information to get out to parents, call the first person on the list and relay the information. Have that parent write down the information, then call the next person on the list. The last parent on the list calls you so you know that everyone got the message. To avoid breakdowns, have anyone who isn't able to contact the next parent on the list call you. You can decide whether you want the parent to keep trying to contact that parent or to skip to another parent. Then you can contact the uninformed parents.

● When your group is on a trip, designate one parent at home as the contact person to relay information to and from the kids. Make sure your contact person has the names and phone numbers of all the parents as well as the phone numbers and itinerary for your trip.

Transportation Coordinators

Recruit mechanically inclined parents and parents who have good organizational skills to work as "transportation ministers" who coordinate all your group's transportation needs. Depending on their skills, these parents can divide the responsibilities for recruiting drivers for trips, renting vans and trailers when needed, arranging for vehicle maintenance and repair, and so on.

Trip Sponsors

Your adult volunteers can get worn out just covering your regular youth group transportation needs, and special trips and events can sometimes push them over the edge.

To avoid volunteer burnout, recruit other parents to serve as "trip sponsors" for specific trips your youth group takes.

Have these trip sponsors take responsibility for different aspects of the trips. For example, different sponsors can take care of communication needs (including announcements and phone calls), collect any signatures needed from parents (such as on permission forms), or monitor budget concerns (including coordinating fund-raisers, planning meals and buying food, and making reservations). They could also arrange transportation (including the actual loading and unloading of vehicles, as well as vehicle rental and driving), or volunteer as an adult leaders for the trip.

Youth Group Volunteer Leader

The most obvious way to involve parents in the spiritual and social growth of the kids in your ministry is to recruit parents to help lead your regular youth group meetings. Parents could help lead in any one of these ways.

● Ask parents to be Bible study teachers for midweek programs. Parents can prepare studies around youth issues, choose passages from Scripture, and help kids see the relevance for today, or choose themes tied to the youth meetings or the pastor's sermons. Make Bible commentaries available to parents so they'll feel more comfortable with Scripture passages, but encourage parents to have kids discuss and make sense of passages for themselves. Parents can also use Group's *Active Bible Curriculum®* series for junior and senior highers as Bible study resources.

● Recruit parents to be discussion group leaders. Divide your youth group into small discussion groups during part of your program for more intimate exploration and discovery of Bible lessons. Place a parent in each small group to facilitate the discussion. (Remind parents not to monopolize the conversation.) Using small groups gives more kids a chance to ask questions and express themselves.

Encourage parents to ask open-ended questions and to help kids open up about their feelings and opinions. For example, "How did you feel when...?" Have parents take discussions to a deeper level by using follow-up questions such as "What do you mean by...?" "What reasons do you have?" or "How did you decide...?" Remind parents to wait for students' answers (thinking takes time) and to encourage students' questions.

● Ask parents to serve as "on-call" substitutes. Some parents who can't make a commitment to come every week are willing to commit to an "as needed and available basis." Invite substitutes to attend your volunteer-training program so they're familiar with your philosophy and curriculum.

PARENT SUPPORT GROUPS

Parenting is difficult. While trying to satisfy so many commitments, parents often burn the midnight oil until they feel like nothing more than smoldering wicks. Parents need help, and that help can come in the form of parent support groups at your church. When parents come together, they can rekindle one another's energy and enthusiasm. Parent groups also help parents see how much they have in common with other parents—and how much their kids have in common with other kids. Parents can draw on one another's strengths to meet one another's needs and discuss how to meet their kids' needs.

Youth ministers usually have many responsibilities and little time to run parent groups. However, you'll probably find a lot of parents at your church want a parent support group and are eager to help start one. Help parents get started, then let them take over the coordination of a vibrant, healthy support group. And when parents are healthy, kids have a better chance of remaining emotionally healthy as well.

Follow these steps to develop a team of parents to coordinate parent support groups in your church.

▼ ▼ ▼ ▼ ▼ ▼ ▼ ▼ ▼ ▼ ▼ ▼ ▼ ▼ ▼ ▼ ▼ ▼

Step 1: THE INTEREST LETTER

Send a letter to a select group of parents asking them to help lead a Parent Ministry Team. Choose parents you admire and would enjoy working with. Include all kinds of parents: single, step, and traditional. Use the "Parent-Ministry-Team Letter to Parents" on page 33 or write one of your own.

Step 2: INTEREST LETTER FOLLOW-UP

Prior to the initial meeting, follow up each letter with a phone call. Determine parents' interest level and answer any questions they may have. Use this sample script when you call:

Hi, (parent's name). **I'm excited about the Parent Ministry Team we're putting together. I'd appreciate your prayerful consideration about being a part of the team. You would give the team excellent direction. I'm calling to confirm the first meeting. It will be** (day and date) **at** (time) **in** (location). **We'll give you more information and answer your questions at the meeting. I'm looking forward to seeing you there.**

Step 3: THE FIRST PMT MEETING

At the first meeting, include a brief time for introductions and an explanation of why parent support groups are needed. Explain that your goal is to create a parent support network that enables parents to help each other deal with the stress of parenting teenagers. Let everyone know that you'd like the people on the Parent Ministry Team to be the leaders and coordinators of this network.

Next, form groups of up to three people each and ask groups to discuss these questions:

● **What would you like to see happen in a parent support network?**

● **How would you word a mission statement (or a one-sentence summary of the goal) for a parent support network?**

• **What needs of parents would you say are most pressing for a parent support network to address?**

Have a representative from each trio report the results of his or her group's discussion. Then have the group as a whole develop a mission statement to guide future efforts and prioritize the top five needs they'd like the parent support network to address.

Set a date for a second meeting. Tell parents you'd like each of them to consider overseeing one program that meets one of the five needs they've listed as their top priorities. Tell them that at the next meeting you'll ask them each to identify the one area they'd like to work with. Any need not selected at this time will be considered only when a volunteer expresses an interest in working with it. Assure parents that you'll help them, but *they* will be the leaders for their area of concern in the parent support network.

Step 4: | AFTER THE FIRST PMT MEETING

No later than two business days after the meeting, mail a brief summary of the things discussed at the meeting to the parents who attended. A few days before the second meeting, call parents to see if they have any further questions.

Step 5: | THE SECOND PMT MEETING

At the second meeting, open with a brief devotion. For devotion ideas, check out *Communication: Enhancing Your Relationships* or *The Church: What Am I Doing Here?* from Group's *Apply-It-to-Life™ Adult Bible Series*. Review the summary of the first meeting. Then give parents a chance to identify areas of need they'd be willing to coordinate.

Have everyone brainstorm ways to meet the top five needs identified at the previous meeting. Then brainstorm specific ideas for each area that parents volunteer to coordinate. If no one volunteers for a certain need, that's OK. Keep that area of need on the back burner for consideration at a later date.

Have parents who volunteer to work on each of the areas of need get together in separate groups and schedule a time to get together for a planning session. Set a time (at least once a month) for a regular meeting of the entire Parent Ministry

Team. Find out the best times for people to meet, such as breakfast or lunch groups, evening groups for parents who work during the day, and daytime groups for those who work nights or prefer day meetings.

Then set the Parent Ministry Team loose to create new programs, plans, and ideas for the parent support network. Encourage parents to plan practical projects that can be done as a ministry to other parents. For example, some people on the Parent Ministry Team may want to start a weekly parent's Bible study during the midweek youth group meetings. Others may want to create a parents' prayer line. Still others may want to coordinate a monthly event for families with teenagers. Ask each team to develop a plan to meet the specific needs they volunteered for and to be ready to implement that plan.

One other option, though it's not required, is to elect officers for the Parent Ministry Team. For example, elect a president who coordinates communication and leads group meetings, a facilities coordinator who helps work out how facilities and resources are shared among those involved in the parent support network, and a secretary who publishes a monthly newsletter with updates and pertinent information about the support network.

Step 6: ALL PARENTS NIGHT

When the Parent Ministry Team is ready to put its plans and programs into action, host a well-publicized "All Parents Night." This is a meeting for parents of kids in your youth ministry to come together to learn about the parent support groups that will be offered. During this meeting, give parents an opportunity to sign up to participate in the parent support network.

Make this a fun time with refreshments and games. Also include a question-and-answer time so everyone can learn more about the issues they're unsure of.

Step 7: AVOID COMMON PITFALLS

When the parent support groups are rolling, you'll want to avoid any situations that could lead to an abrupt end to all your great plans. Here are just a few things to watch out for.

● **Gripe sessions**—This happens when groups have no

specific direction or common focus or when meetings have no time limit. Rather than sharing positive ideas, these groups quickly become complaint sessions. The meeting agenda can be flexible, but be sure to have a set focus such as a specific topic to discuss or a book to read. Encourage groups to set ending times as well as beginning times.

● **Dominating participants**—Some people who participate in a support group tend to monopolize the time. Make sure everyone has a chance to be heard, supported, and encouraged.

● **Individualized situations**—Avoid spending a lot of time on problems that are so individualized the rest of the group members don't benefit.

● **Low trust level**—You need to build an atmosphere of openness and honesty, otherwise parents may cover up real problems and deal only with surface issues while appearing to have everything in control.

Step 8: | STAY FLEXIBLE

For each group to fulfill its potential benefit, you'll need to make minor adjustments after the group's initial formation. Here are some suggestions to help you avoid drastic problems later.

● **Select a group name that communicates excitement and energy.** The term "support group" may have negative connotations for some. Instead, call your group a Parent Affirmation Group, Parent Sharing Group, Parent Idea Bank, or something similar.

● **Limit the time commitment.** Six or eight weeks is a good time span for a group. If the group members decide to continue, have them agree to another six- or eight-week period.

● **Have a focus.** Use a film or tape series, speaker series, a seminar, a workshop, or study a book on parenting. Several books to consider are Merton and Irene Strommen's *Five Cries of Parents,* Gregg and Margie Lewis' *The Hurting Parent,* Carol Kuykendall's *Learning to Let Go,* and Richard and Renee Durfield's *Raising Them Chaste.* Two videos to consider are *Learn to Discern: Help for a Generation at Risk* and *Children at Risk* (check your local Christian bookstore to find these resources).

● **Train your leaders.** Make sure leaders are familiar with small group dynamics and can facilitate the sharing. Consider leading the first meeting to model good group leadership for the leaders. It's important to continue training your leaders. If you have a psychologist or counselor in your church, ask him or her to train your leaders.

Step 9: | SUPPORTING THE SUPPORT GROUP LEADERS

The leaders of your parent support group will be dealing with individuals who are coming together to learn and to share their own situations. Productive meetings are crucial to reaching that goal. Pass suggestions along ahead of time to each parent who will lead a support group meeting. Give each support group leader a photocopy of the "Leading a Parent Support Group" handout on page 34 to use as a reference.

Step 10: | EVALUATION

Set regular times to meet with leaders to evaluate the effectiveness of the support groups. It might be necessary to change the goals, the leaders, or the content of the meetings.

Go through the pitfalls listed in the "Step 7: Avoid Common Pitfalls" paragraph on page 30. Brainstorm suggestions to help the leaders of groups that are falling into these pitfalls. Discuss the focus of each group and whether or not that focus needs to shift. Talk about attendance. If attendance is low in a group, try to figure out why; for example, is it because meetings don't start and end on time, a person in the group controls and dominates discussions, or someone criticizes or frequently gives unsolicited advice instead of affirming other members?

Close the meetings with prayer for the leaders and the groups.

PARENT-MINISTRY-TEAM LETTER TO PARENTS

Dear

A recent study confirms that communication between parents and children is poorest during the teenage years. I probably don't need to tell you that. Or that these conditions cause stress for the entire family.

That's why I believe a successful youth ministry includes not only young people but also parents and families. To help address these needs, I am forming a Parent Ministry Team (PMT).

The PMT would meet monthly and oversee a network of parent support groups. The PMT would be responsible for identifying the needs of parents in our congregation and planning and implementing ways to meet those needs. For example, the PMT might coordinate a parents' newsletter to educate parents about current youth issues. Or it might sponsor a study series on parenting or put on quarterly seminars and workshops for parents to help them grow in parenting skills. To encourage parent-teenager communication, the PMT could start combined parents-and-kids activities on a regular basis.

As you can see, the possibilities are endless. With an active team of 10 to 12 adults, no one person would be overwhelmed, and many good things will happen.

I'm writing to ask you to consider serving on the PMT. We can all benefit from your concern for effective parenting and your love for young people. I believe you'd offer excellent direction for this new branch of our ministry, and I hope you'll consider this position with much thought and prayer.

The first meeting will be _____ at _____. I'll be contacting you in the next few days about the meeting.

Sincerely,

LEADING A PARENT SUPPORT GROUP

Follow these tips to help you conduct a successful parent support group in your church.

● Always use name tags! Have parents print their names in large letters.

● Spend a brief time at each session allowing parents to get to know each other better. Here's a good icebreaker: Hand out a piece of paper and a pencil to each person. Ask group members to each recall something humorous that happened to them when they were teenagers. Have them write these down without identifying themselves, then fold their papers. Collect the papers, then redistribute them. Have parents read the papers one at a time, with the group guessing whose story was just read. This not only helps the group members get to know each other better, but also lets them reflect on how they acted as teenagers.

● Briefly summarize the youth ministry activities of the previous week. This enables the parents to "get on board" at the meeting.

● Help parents look at the good side. Here's an effective exercise. First, have parents list their most cherished traits of childhood; for example, carefree, playful, and free. Then have them list the traits of a successful adult; for example, hard-working, self-controlled, and responsible. Finally, ask them to list the characteristics of a highly stressed adult; for example, on edge, hyperactive, and withdrawn. This exercise is valuable because it gives parents a new perspective on their kids. It helps them see the difference between building successful kids with normal childhood traits and prematurely turning kids into adults by stressing characteristics from the second list.

● Be sensitive to parents' reactions. Some members of the group may not feel comfortable opening up to everyone. You'll want the group's openness to increase with time. But if you notice the discussion getting uncomfortable for group members, don't be afraid to move on to a less-threatening topic.

● Take every opportunity to affirm parents. They're trying hard and need positive strokes.

● Summarize each session with specific recommendations for more effective parenting.

● Close with a brief prayer of thanks for the kids and for the parents who care enough about their kids to be part of such a group.

PART 2

BRINGING
Parents and Kids
TOGETHER

ADVENTURES AND ACTIVITIES FOR PARENTS AND TEENAGERS

Some days the only time parents and kids see each other is when they're dashing through dinner. Your youth group can become another place for parents' and kids' lives to merge—for them to have fun together and try on each other's shoes.

Having fun together can calm the fears that often keep parents and kids from sharing the real stuff—their hurts, pains, disappointments, and victories. Just being together may spark meaningful conversations. The discussion starters following some of the activities can also encourage communication between parents and kids as they discuss feelings, discoveries, and the good and bad of the experience. Even the most hesitant will get interested as they see their friends' positive results.

Boost participation and enthusiasm by sending special invitations to parents and kids to remind them and encourage them to be part of your parents-and-kids social activities.

Here are some ideas for fun ways to involve parents with the kids in your group. Use these friendly activities to strengthen the relationships between parents and kids.

▼ ▼ ▼ ▼ ▼ ▼ ▼ ▼ ▼ ▼ ▼ ▼ ▼ ▼ ▼ ▼ ▼ ▼ ▼

Adapting a Youth Group Meeting

You can use any youth group meeting as a parents-and-kids meeting. Invite parents to join your group at its weekly meeting. Plan and run the meeting as you normally would, allowing time at the end for discussion. End the meeting by talking through the discussion starters.

Discussion starters:
- What can parents and kids learn from one another about God?
- What did you learn about each other during the meeting?
- What are other topics you think would be good to explore in a meeting that includes both parents and teenagers?

A Birthday Switch

Encourage parents to walk in their teenagers' shoes. Have parents attend the youth group meeting in place of their kids the week their kids have a birthday. There are many benefits to this switch. The teenager gets some quiet time at home, and the parent experiences what it's like to belong to a youth group. Parents will have a greater understanding of what you do and will be even more supportive. When parents attend, urge them to participate in every aspect of the meeting, even the games! If you're in the habit of celebrating kids' birthdays, be sure to celebrate their birthdays the preceding or following week.

Spotlight parents who attend your meeting by having them each tell a story about their first day with their child. This may be birth, adoption, or dating stories depending on the circumstances. Be sensitive to family situations.

Note: Another option is to have both the teenager and the parent attend the meeting. In this case, have the teenager join with the parent throughout the evening.

The Complete Picture

Try this idea to help kids and parents communicate.

Create fliers to advertise an upcoming event for kids and parents, such as a family picnic or parent-teenager date night. Then cut the fliers in half. Send half of the flier to parents and the other half to kids. To get the complete message, kids and parents have to put their halves together! This makes people aware of the event and also forces them to communicate.

Croquet or Bowling Tournament

Hold a croquet or bowling tournament for kids and their parents. Both of these games are easygoing and fun, even for the inexperienced or unathletic. Form family teams or play kids vs. parents. Present a silly trophy to the winning team, such as a twisted wicket or a helium balloon decorated as a bowling ball. Follow up by gathering everyone together and reading Jesus' statement about the last being first in Luke 13:30. Form small groups with parents and kids in each group. Have groups use the following discussion starters to spark conversation.

Discussion starters:
● How does this Scripture compare to values you see demonstrated in our society?
● How does this Scripture apply to you?
● What's the value of competition?
● What's the value of relationships with friends and family?
● Is winning ever more important than your relationship with your competitor?
● How can you be competitive and still be a friend?

Family Carnival

Here's a chance for parents to see the fun side of youth ministry. Have your youth group sponsor a family carnival. Have kids plan and staff various booths and activities for their families. Try these ideas.

● **Soaking-Sponge Throw**—Set up a booth where parents get three chances to throw a soaking-wet sponge at a teenage target.

● **Memory Lane Photo Booth**—Give each family an opportunity to receive a free, instant-print family picture. For fun, provide props and costumes for families to wear, such as old-fashioned clothes or Western wear.

● **Parents' Dessert Bake-Off**—Sponsor a dessert competition. Have parents (moms or dads) enter homemade desserts. Select a panel of teenagers to act as judges.

● **Skill Games**—Offer a variety of skill games for families to play, such as basketball throws, beanbag tosses, and milk-carton knockdowns.

Family Fun Nights

Have fellowship and fun nights for families, centered around activities such as skating, shopping, and hayrides. Encourage each family to stick together and mingle with other families. After the activities, gather at the church, a restaurant, someone's home, or around a campfire. Use the discussion starters to talk about how families relate.

Discussion starters:
● How does it feel to laugh and relax with your family?
● How do you feel when you're in public with your family?
● What's something new you learned about each other tonight?

● What did you find out you liked about your family that you didn't know before?

Invitational Snow-Sculpting Contest

If you live in a place where it snows during the winter, gather parents and kids in a large snowy field or park—the more public the place the better. (If you live where no snow is available, substitute ice, dirt, or sand for the contest.) Form teams by mixing youth group members with parents.

Then invite parents and kids to start forming anything out of the snow. Have contests for the most creative or the most likely to appear in an art museum.

If you want more snow fun, form two teams and let each team build a fort or wall. Then bombard each other with snowballs.

Invite the public to this sculpting-bombarding event by leaving large messages around your church and town written in the snow. Use food coloring and water in a squirt bottle to write your messages or "foot stomp" the messages in the snow.

Roving Christmas Caroling Party

Have kids and parents gather in your youth group meeting room after your regular church Christmas party, then proceed to a mall. Sing a carol or two, then go on to another public place, such as a restaurant or theater, sing a carol or two, and so on, until you get back to your church.

Design and take along a colorful poster board sign that says which church you're from and invites people to join in with you. Even if they don't join you now, they'll remember you as people who have a lot of fun!

A Night at the Movies

Invite parents and kids to attend a movie together. Pick a film that is intriguing both to kids and adults. (Don't underestimate kids' interests.) After the movie, go to the church for popcorn and to critique the film and its message. Finish the discussion by telling kids and parents that, flawed as we are, God doesn't allow some critic to determine whether or not we are acceptable to him.

If you want to add some more character-building and controversy to your meetings, try "A Night at the Movies" discussions using the following discussion starters.

Discussion starters:

● How are the characters' religious beliefs, morality, ethics, and sense of responsibility similar to or different from yours?

● What kinds of movies do you like to watch?

● Does what a movie is rated affect whether you choose to watch it? Explain.

● How does material that causes R ratings add or detract from movie plots?

● Does Hollywood sensationalize or portray reality? Explain.

● Is Hollywood biased? Explain.

● Do Hollywood producers and directors need to be more responsible about what kinds of movies they make?

● Should movies be censored? Why or why not?

Wrap up the activity by having parents talk about what movies were like when they were teenagers and when their parents were teenagers.

Picture Perfect

Use this adaptation of the game Pictionary to help parents and teenagers explore the topic of communication.

Form teams of 10 to 15. Make sure there are parents and kids on each team. Use newsprint or an erasable board for the drawings. You can even make up your own "Church" category with words such as "Bible" and "pastor" to throw into the game on All Plays. After the game is finished, use the discussion starters to talk about communication.

Discussion starters:

● Why was it hard to guess what some of the pictures were?

● Why is it sometimes hard to get someone to understand your side of an argument?

● Why do parents and kids sometimes have different opinions about what's important?

● How can our experiences and prejudices affect how we see something?

● How do you resolve a conflict?

● When is it OK to compromise and when is it not OK?
● What steps can we take to communicate more effectively?

Close the discussion by giving parents and kids the "Mind Your P's and Q's" handout on page 46 and having them do the communication exercise on the handout together.

Reverse-Roles Progressive Dinner

Plan a progressive dinner for parents and kids. A progressive dinner is when participants travel from house to house, eating a different course of the menu at each stop. For example, at the first house everyone might eat soup, then travel to a second house for salad, a third house for a main dish, and so on.

Have kids do all the cooking and chaperone their parents from house to house. Limit dinner groups to four families. After dinner, talk about the reversal of roles, that is, kids serving their parents. Have all the families meet at the church at a designated time. Use the discussion starters to talk about the experience.

Discussion starters:
● How did it feel to play reversed parent (child) roles?
● When have you helped family members without being asked?
● What are ways you can help your family members?
● How do kids and parents take each other for granted?
● What makes parents feel unappreciated by kids?
● What makes kids feel unappreciated by parents?
● Why is it hard sometimes to balance giving and receiving?

Risk Tournament

Gather several games of Risk and let kids play to introduce a discussion on the topic of power. The purpose of Risk is to conquer the world. To do that you have to take risks. Discuss risk-taking in families and the power struggles families go through.

Discussion starters:
● Who won the game? Why?
● Why was aggressive play important?
● What risks did you take during the game?

- What did this game teach you about people?
- Did you enjoy conquering your opponent? Why or why not?
- What are ways you try to defeat each other in family relationships?
- What are good risks you should take in your families?

Scavenger Hunt

Form teams that have both parents and kids. Use a mall, an airport, or a neighborhood as the setting for a one-hour scavenger hunt. Give each team a list of 25 or so items to find. For example, your list might include things like "an item from a grocery store," "something red," "a soft drink can," "something with stripes," and so on. Tailor your list to the area you'll be using for this activity. After the scavenger hunt, gather at a group member's home for refreshments and discussion.

Discussion starters:
- Who ended up taking charge of the group? Why?
- How much did the kids on your team lead?
- What were some of the ways you had fun together?
- What was the most interesting thing that happened?

Supper Dialogues

Invite parents and kids to go out for pizza or have a dinner at the church. Seat a couple of parents and a couple of kids at each table. Use these groupings of parents and kids for small group discussions.

Discussion starters for kids to ask parents:
- How did you know when you were in love?
- How did you decide what you wanted for a career?
- What have been times you've doubted God?
- When have you had trouble with friendships?
- How can kids keep from letting parents down?

Discussion starters for parents to ask kids:
- When have you had trouble with friendships?
- What have been times you've doubted God?
- Where do you see yourself five years from now?
- What qualities do you think are important in a husband or wife?
- How can parents keep from letting kids down?

After dinner have a feedback session at the church for kids and parents to talk about what they've learned.

Trivia Bowl

Gather parents and kids for games of Trivial Pursuit. Try parents-and-kids teams or parents vs. kids. If you run out of time to finish games, give teams a final Bible trivia question, such as what Persian queen was adopted as a child? (Esther) Whoever answers first wins. If no one answers, call it a tie. Afterward, use the discussion starters to start a conversation about how we learn and stay informed.

Discussion starters:
● Where have you learned about history, science, and literature?
● Where have you learned about God?
● How did you find out which TV programs, movies, or books you'd like?
● How do you find out about current events and discoveries?
● How do you think our understanding and opinions can be affected if we don't hear all the facts and both sides of a story?
● How much do you trust the information you get from newspapers, magazines, radio, and television?
● What recent events, discoveries, literature, entertainment, and so on do you think will be remembered and taught to the next generation?

Video/Film Festival

Bring parents and kids together at the church to watch and discuss a video or film. Provide popcorn, soft drinks, Milk Duds, M&M's, and other favorite movie treats. And don't forget the VCR and television or projector and screen.

Here are some movies to generate discussion between parents and kids:

Secular videos—

Joe Versus the Volcano (Rated PG), *Dead Poets Society* (Rated PG), *Awakenings* (Rated PG-13), *Cry Freedom* (Rated PG), *Places in the Heart* (Rated PG), *Stand and Deliver* (Rated PG), *The Chosen* (Rated PG), *Chariots of Fire* (Rated PG), *Ghandi* (Rated PG), *E.T.* (Rated PG), *On Golden Pond* (Rated PG), *The*

Color Purple (Rated PG-13), *Fried Green Tomatoes* (Rated PG-13), *My Girl* (Rated PG), *The Elephant Man* (Rated PG), *Man Without a Face* (Rated PG-13), *Boyz N the Hood* (Rated R), and *Schindler's List* (Rated R).

Note: Some of the movies above contain material that might be inappropriate in your youth group setting. Be sure to preview any movie before showing it to your kids and get input from parents regarding the movies you choose to show.

Christian videos and films—
From Mars Hill Productions, Inc., (713) 240-6474—*Moment of Truth, Without Reservation, Future Tense, The Question, One in a Million, The Biggest and the Best.*
From Focus on the Family, (719) 531-3495—*Twice Pardoned.*
From Gospel Films, Inc., 800-253-0413—*Thin Ice, Dravecky: A Story of Courage & Grace, A Man Called Norman.*
From Group Publishing, Inc., 800-447-1070—*Hot Talk-Starter Video Series.*

To order a Christian film, call your local Christian bookstore or film distributor. To show a secular video, make sure you order the video through a company that offers public performance rights. Two such companies are Films, Inc., P.M.I. at 800-323-4222 and Swank Motion Pictures at 800-876-5577.

Use the discussion starters or put together more specific questions to get kids and parents to think about the film's message.

Discussion starters:
● Which character did you most identify with?
● Which character did you least identify with?
● What did these characters do right?
● What did they do wrong?
● What would you have done differently if you were in these characters' situations?
● What events were turning points in these characters' lives?
● How did these events make you feel?
● What perspectives or insights into life did you pick up?
● What else did you learn from this film?
● What will you do or think about differently after viewing this film?

MIND YOUR P'S AND Q'S

Read the communication tip below. Then describe to your partner a picture or poster that's hanging on a wall in your home. Practice using "P's" and "Q's" while you discuss a picture or poster with each other.

Afterward, join with another pair to form a foursome and discuss how effective you were in communicating the information regarding your chosen pictures to each other.

Here's a tip to help you communicate more effectively:

Always respond to what the other person has said. The best way to respond is to mind your P's and Q's throughout a conversation.

"P" stands for *paraphrase.* Say the other person's comments in your own words. If you misunderstood, the other person has a chance to correct you.

"Q" stands for *questions.* Ask the other person questions about what's been said. This helps clarify any statements that were unclear to you or the person to whom you're speaking.

SERVICE PROJECTS FOR PARENTS AND TEENAGERS

Working side by side on a service project is a nonthreatening way for parents and kids to spend time together building relationships. Doing a project together gives them many opportunities to talk informally and get to know each other better. A lot of bonding can take place, too, during the special moments that happen when people help other people. Working on service projects also builds team spirit and develops the qualities it takes to be a team player. Through service projects, parents and kids can build character and memories, as well as get the chance to live out their faith.

If you use project coordinators for the ideas in this chapter, make sure the coordinators *coordinate* rather than *dominate*. Let kids and parents organize and work on the service projects together. This builds cooperation and camaraderie since everyone is working on the same level. It also gives kids dignity and self-esteem and parents a respect for the kids.

▼ ▼ ▼ ▼ ▼ ▼ ▼ ▼ ▼ ▼ ▼ ▼ ▼ ▼ ▼ ▼ ▼ ▼ ▼

Angel Tree Ornaments

Your parents and kids will experience great satisfaction during the Christmas holiday by ministering to prisoners' children through the Prison Fellowship Angel Tree project. Prison Fellowship provides a list of children and their needs—such as clothing and toys.

After selecting a name, parents and kids work together to purchase items for that child. The gifts are then given on behalf of the prisoner-parent and in the name of Jesus. Presents need to be sent in time to be delivered in mid-December.

For more information about the Angel Tree program, contact Prison Fellowship, Box 17500, Washington, DC 20041-0500, (703) 478-0100.

Here are a couple of ideas on how parents and kids can work together to provide presents for the Angel Tree project.

Shopping Trip—Secure money from your church's outreach fund or hold a fund-raiser, such as the "Faithful Flea Market" described on page 50, to cover the cost of gifts. Let parents and kids know as early as possible about how much money they'll have to spend.

Gather parents and kids at the church. Have parents bring wrapping paper, tape, and scissors. Pick a shopping mall for the spree. Before the trip, form groups with a couple of parents and a couple of kids in each group. If applicable, give each group its portion of the outreach money. Provide each group a child's name and a list of his or her needs to shop for. Choose a time and place to rendezvous at the mall after shopping. Then head for the mall in a caravan.

After shopping, have everyone meet at the appointed place and time and head back to the church in a caravan. Gather at the church to wrap the gifts. Have groups share the wrapping paper supplies. Provide hot chocolate, eggnog, and cookies.

Angel Tree—Near mid-November, set up a Christmas tree in a visible place in your church, such as the foyer. Have parents and kids decorate the tree with a paper angel for each child. Have church families choose "angels" and purchase the suggested presents.

Collect the presents at the beginning of December and have a gift-wrapping party at the church with parents and kids. Have parents bring wrapping paper, tape, and scissors from home. Provide hot chocolate, Christmas cookies, and eggnog.

Assembly-Line Gift Kits

Reach out to others at Christmas (or any time of the year) by getting your youth group to assemble gift kits of food or clothing.

Announce to your church that your youth ministry's parents and kids are collecting items to help the needy. Invite church members to bring their items to the church. Or have parents and kids go door to door collecting items in their neighborhoods.

Then organize an assembly-line packing day. Group similar items in piles along the tables. Assign a person to each pile. Start a box at one end and pass it from person to person, each putting in the assigned item. Besides boxing canned food for families or toys for kids, try some of these ideas:

● **Baby items**—Prepare and deliver individual boxes for new moms or children's homes. Assemble boxes of blankets, diapers, washcloths, powder, clothes, and booties.

● **Winter clothes**—Contact the Salvation Army or another local organization that reaches out to needy families. Choose a couple of families to help. Find out clothing sizes and the number of people in each family. Prepare and deliver boxes with mittens, scarves, hats, coats, and warm socks.

● **Office supplies**—Contact your pastor for names and addresses of local nonprofit organizations or missionaries who have an ongoing need for office supplies. Write or call those organizations or missionaries to find out exactly what they need, then gather and send Bibles, paper, pencils, erasers, pens, tape, paper clips, rulers, hole punches, scissors, stamps, and envelopes to meet their needs.

● **School supplies**—Call your denomination's main office for mission school addresses. Then contact the mission schools to find out what they need for school supplies. Prepare and send individual boxes of paper, pencils, erasers, blunt-end scissors, crayons, and rulers as requested to meet the needs of the schools.

Add a finishing touch to each box by gift wrapping it and attaching a card signed by parents and kids.

Children in Hospitals

Entertain and visit patients in local children's hospitals or wards. Call the hospital's volunteer coordinator to make arrangements. Throw parties, if permissible. Bring balloons.

Have a story time or a skit. Pair up parents with kids and have pairs visit rooms to read stories and talk with children. Or dress parents and kids up as clowns—most children love clowns. For tips on clowning, use the book *Clown Ministry* by Floyd Shaffer and Penne Sewell (available from Group Publishing).

Christmas Stocking Project

Your parents and kids can make a difference for inner-city children by teaming up with Metro Assembly of God in Brooklyn, New York—a church that ministers to over 10,000 children.

Using green or red felt and a pattern provided by Metro Assembly of God, parents and kids can sew Christmas stockings and stuff the stockings with suggested treats. For many children the stocking may be the only Christmas present they receive.

Metro must receive completed stockings by November 30. To order patterns and instructions, write: Metro Assembly of God, Box 370695, Brooklyn, NY 11237-0015.

Designer Outreach Cards

Have parents and kids bring in names and addresses of new people in the church, elderly neighbors, or people they know who are shut-ins at home, or in a hospital, nursing home, prison, or other institution.

Have parents and kids (the "designers") create cards out of items such as construction paper, glitter, scraps of wrapping paper, yarn, stickers, fabric, wallpaper scraps, and so on. Have designers write appropriate greetings, such as seasonal messages at Christmas and Easter or encouraging messages and reminders of God's love in any season. Also write a note about your youth group and church. Then have all the parents and kids sign the cards. Send the cards and watch the responses you'll get.

A Faithful Flea Market

Earn money for outreach by having parents and kids host an indoor flea market at your church or another suitable facility.

Invite church families to gather goods to sell, such as crafts, clothes, games, utensils, and baked goods. Arrange tables in a fellowship hall or large gymnasium. Charge families a flat rental fee for their space or 10 percent of their proceeds, to be collected at the end of the day. Put the money in your church's outreach fund, the Angel Tree project on page 48, the Christmas Stocking project on page 50, or other designated project.

Have your youth group sell Kool-Aid, popcorn, fruit, and cookies. All proceeds go to your outreach project.

Advertise the sale in your local newspaper as well as in your church bulletin and newsletter. Hand out fliers giving details about your church services and programs. Not only will you reach out to the needy, you'll reach out to unchurched local people who attend your flea market.

Food Pantries

Arrange for parents and kids to work with a local food pantry. Check with your church office for a listing of food pantries in your area. Call the pantries to find out what their needs are right now. Food pantries often need help with distribution, putting food on the shelves, picking up food, or unloading vehicles.

Furniture and Clothing

Agencies that give away clothes and furniture often need help picking up the items, unloading trucks, warehousing, and even delivering goods. Two agencies that give away furniture and clothes are the Salvation Army and St. Vincent De Paul Society. Your church office may have a listing of other agencies. If not, look under "Social Service Organizations" in your Yellow Pages.

Gifts for the Homeless

Call a homeless shelter director or other local organization that works with people on the street to find out about giving Christmas gifts to homeless people. Since shelter residents are often transient, you may need to buy more general gift items such as one-size-fits-all socks, hats, or gloves. Find out what toys would be appropriate. You can also set up a program with local children's homes or halfway houses and give birthday presents to their residents on a regular basis.

Holiday Food

Turkey and the trimmings can transform someone's holiday season. Some agencies and food pantries have people come in to pick up food, other places deliver it. And still others actually cook the food and serve a meal. Check with your local food pantries and agencies. Then give parents and kids a chance to make the holidays special for a lot of people.

Home Repair

Some elderly, handicapped, and low-income people live in houses that have deteriorated over the years. Parents and kids can build houses or make houses fit to live in again. Repairing and building houses is usually a very rewarding experience for both parents and kids. Group Workcamps has summer programs geared specifically for youth group kids, parents, and volunteers; contact them at 800-635-0404. Habitat for Humanity has spring break work parties; contact them at 800-422-4828. Or contact your local weatherization program.

Nursing Home Parties

Most nursing home residents and staff enjoy any kind of socializing. Call the activity director at a nursing home to see if you can throw a party for the residents. Think of a reason for the party, such as Christmas, Valentine's Day, Groundhog Day, or a "special-people" party. Serve punch and cookies. Let some of the parents and kids show off their musical talents to entertain the residents.

Nursing Home Sing-Alongs

Recruit a musician or ensemble. Have parents and kids learn some vintage songs or old gospel hymns. Then take the act on the road to your local nursing home. Ask a nursing home activity director to schedule you for a sing-along. If you need a piano or organ, ask if the home has one; if not, take a portable keyboard.

Prisons

Many ministries visit prisons, such as Prison Fellowship, Box 17500, Washington, DC 20041-0500, (703) 478-0100. See what's available in your area and plug into an existing program. If you want to start your own program, consult with a current ministry so you know what to do and what to expect.

Safehouses for Abused Women and Children

In the rush to escape, victims of abuse usually leave a lot of belongings behind. Safehouses usually don't publish their addresses or phone numbers. Call a local social-service agency to get in touch with a safehouse. Find out what the families need, such as clothes, diapers, gift certificates for haircuts, or bus passes. Find ways to meet those needs.

Shelter Maintenance and Repairs

Sometimes homeless shelters don't have the staff or money to keep up their facilities. Offer your help to shelter directors. Parents and kids can paint or make minor repairs and organize clothes closets. Shelter residents often fight discouragement. Don't underestimate the influence a neat and clean facility can have on people's spirits and self-esteem.

Shut-In, Nursing Home, and Hospital Visits

From your pastor or church secretary, get a list of church members who are in either a hospital or a nursing home or are shut-in. You can also put an announcement in the church bulletin to find out if church members have family or friends that need someone to visit. Pair up parents with kids. Have pairs visit the people on the list. After you get the names, call first to make sure it's OK to visit, then find out when visiting hours are. Pairs can talk or read to patients. Patients who have had eye surgery or have failing eyesight may need someone to read their mail to them. Parents and kids can even pray with patients who want to be prayed with.

Being alone and unable to get around at Christmas is doubly hard. Check with chaplains or volunteer coordinators to see if there are any programs your kids and parents can participate in to assist these needy persons. Or start an outreach of your own.

Yardwork and Cleaning

Many elderly and disabled people are unable to do their own yardwork or housecleaning. Check with the elderly and disabled in your own church to see who needs help. Send a crew over to transform their homes with floor mopping, window washing, vacuuming, raking, grass cutting, or other chores they need done.

Some people have little family or community support. If parents and kids are brave enough, call an agency that works with the elderly or disabled and offer to clean homes that don't qualify for housecleaning services. These people desperately need this service, but the task is not for the faint-hearted. **Caution:** Some homes may have insects or rodents.

MEETINGS FOR PARENTS AND TEENAGERS

Why don't parents and kids understand each other? It's usually a matter of perspective. Kids are forming relationships, maturing, savoring every moment, and learning to be independent. Parents are deepening relationships, meeting daily obligations, securing their future, and juggling family responsibilities. So parents and kids butt heads because the boundaries of their perspectives rarely cross.

Use these meetings to give parents and kids a chance to walk in each other's shoes and develop empathy for each other's point of view.

▼ ▼ ▼ ▼ ▼ ▼ ▼ ▼ ▼ ▼ ▼ ▼ ▼ ▼ ▼ ▼ ▼ ▼ ▼

MEETING 1: A Family-Ties Surprise

Use this meeting to help teenagers and their parents see things from each other's perspective, work through problems from a new vantage point, and to encourage them to appreciate one another.

Objectives

Parents and kids will
● play a blindfold game to discover blind spots that keep them from open communication and compassionate understanding,

● fill out two different charts to help them understand how kids and parents perceive each other,

● play a game patterned after *The Newlywed Game* to help kids and parents talk about the things they struggle to understand about each other, and

● commit to at least one concrete action they can take to promote understanding at home.

Before the Meeting

Read the meeting, collect supplies, and photocopy the handouts.

Invite kids and their parents to the meeting at least one month in advance. If possible, have parents R.S.V.P. so you'll know exactly who'll be there.

Recruit two adult volunteers to ask questions during "The Family-Ties Game" activity on page 58.

Purchase an inexpensive handkerchief or bandanna for each participant. (Or ask kids and parents to each bring a handkerchief or bandanna they can write on, or use strips of an old sheet in place of the bandannas.)

Set up three to five pairs of chairs in the front of the room. Make a sign that reads "The Family-Ties Game" and tape it onto the wall behind the chairs.

Invite others to pray with you for unity between parents and kids.

The Meeting

1. FINDING THE BLINDERS
(up to 15 minutes)

(You'll need a handkerchief or bandanna to use as a blindfold and a marker for each person.) As kids and parents enter, give each a blindfold and a marker. Say: **Write on your blindfold at least 10 areas of "blindness," or lack of understanding, between teenagers and parents. These can be specific areas you fight over at home or ones that are common to all teenagers and parents.**

After 10 minutes or so, tell parents and kids to put on their blindfolds and make sure they can't see. Say: **When I call out a number, I want you to lock arms in a circle of that number of people. Here's the catch: You can't say anything to find each other. For example, if I yell "five," silently find four other people to lock arms with in a circle.**

Call out three or four different numbers, one at a time, and end by calling out the number three. When kids and parents have linked arms in trios, tell participants to remove their blindfolds, sit down in their groups, and discuss the areas of blindness they wrote on their blindfolds.

After a discussion time, ask:

● **How is wearing a blindfold like having a misunderstanding between parents and teenagers?**

Say: **Often when we disagree, we don't understand why the other person doesn't "see" our point. And when we suddenly see a disagreement in a new light, we sometimes try to avoid that new light or put our blindfolds back on. We don't like what we now understand, so we react by saying something that keeps blindfolds up between us. If we choose to, we can take off the blindfolds and use them to clean a hurt or bandage a wound. Put away your blindfolds for now; we'll use them again later.**

2. THE PERCEPTION CONNECTION
(up to 15 minutes)

(You'll need photocopies of the "Quite Apparent" handout on page 60 and "Here's Looking at You, Kid" handout on page 61, pencils, and Bibles.)

Give kids each a pencil and a photocopy of the "Quite Apparent" handout. Give each parent a pencil and a photocopy of the "Here's Looking at You, Kid" handout. Have parents and kids complete each exercise and answer the questions at the end.

After kids and parents finish their handouts, ask a few volunteers to tell about their perceptions. Then have everyone find a partner to discuss these questions:

● **How are our perceptions of each other different today from when kids were 2 years old? 5 years old? 10 years old?**

● **How do teenagers' perceptions of parents and parents' perceptions of teenagers differ?** (For example, parents might consider their kids to be children, but kids may see themselves as more grown up.)

Have pairs read Ephesians 4:29–5:2 and summarize the theme of the passage in one sentence. Then ask pairs:

● **How do our perceptions of each other affect the way we follow or fail to follow the guidelines in Ephesians 4:29–5:2 in regard to our family members?**

● **How can we find out whether our perceptions are right or wrong?**

● **Why is it harder to understand each other now than when kids were younger?**

● What can we do this week to be more understanding with each other?

● How can doing those things help us fulfill the objectives listed in Ephesians 4:29–5:2?

Say: **The more we share our perceptions, fears, hopes, and ideas, the better we understand each other and the better we communicate. Now let's have some fun learning to communicate.**

3. THE FAMILY-TIES GAME
(up to 20 minutes)

(You'll need for each person in the game a marker and nine 8½×11 pieces of construction paper or poster board. You'll also need newsprint and two more markers.)

Ask for three to five parent-teenager pairs to volunteer for the game. Don't pick more than five pairs.

Say: **You've heard of *Family Feud* and *The Newlywed Game.* But today we're going one step further. It's time now for The Family-Ties Game! We'll find out how much teenagers and their parents really know about each other. What bugs them? What do they really like about each other? What's behind their struggles and joys? Let's have our parent-teenager pairs come on up and sit in the game chairs.**

To the people participating in the game, say: **In a moment, you'll leave the room with a leader and privately answer the same questions we'll ask your partner. Then we'll have you come back here to see just how well you know each other.**

Give each participant a marker and nine "cards" (8½×11 pieces of construction paper or poster board). Send the kids participating in the game to one room and the parents to another room. Assign a leader to each group. Give the parents group leader a photocopy of the "Parents" handout (page 62). Give the teenagers group leader a photocopy of the "Teenagers" handout (page 63). Have leaders follow the directions on the handouts.

(**Note:** You may use all or just some of the questions listed but use the same questions for both groups. The questions alternate between affirmation and problem areas.)

While the parent-teenager pairs are out of the room, have the audience form groups of no more than four (mix parents and kids evenly). Give each group newsprint and a marker. Say: **Try to make a long list of "communication clearers" with your group. Communication clearers are ways to take off our blindfolds, to understand each other, and to** encourage each other. **Think of things that would help you live together better at home. You have five minutes.**

Walk around and encourage groups. Tell teams they can list specific issues such as "negotiating curfews" or general principles such as "listening instead of shouting." Encourage creativity and brainstorming.

Call time when leaders tell you the game participants have finished their private answers. Announce that both groups have excellent lists and ask the groups to roll up their lists but don't let anyone see them until you ask for them.

Have the leaders bring in the kids and parents. Have parents and kids sit together in pairs. Have kids complete each sentence the way they think their parents completed the "Parents" handout sentences. After each teenager answers, cue the teenager's parent to lift the card that corresponds with that question. Ask kids each to complete one sentence before moving on to the next one. Encourage applause. Award 20 points for answers that match. For the last two questions, award 40 points for matching answers. Encourage unity by frequently announcing how close the answers were.

Repeat the process with the parents completing the sentences on the "Teenagers" handout.

Encourage sensitivity, surprise, and fun. Point out that we really are alike in our struggles to understand each other. Parents have as much trouble understanding kids as kids do understanding parents. Award the winning pair a free fast-food meal or a "Family-Ties" blue ribbon.

After the game is over and a winner is determined, say: **Parents and teenagers don't always understand each other. To help out, our audience has come up with some ideas to improve your communication and strengthen your ties.**

Before moving on to the next activity, have representatives from each of the audience groups call out ideas from their lists that they think would help the game participants.

4. HEALING THE BLINDNESS
(up to 10 minutes)

Form a circle. Ask parents and kids to take out their handkerchiefs or bandannas from the "Finding the Blinders" activity (p. 56) and circle three areas of blindness they want to remove from their family. Have kids and parents each name an area of blindness and the action they plan to take to remove it. After each person talks, ask everyone to say, "Good idea!" Tell kids and parents to keep their handkerchiefs or bandannas in a prominent place as a reminder of their commitment.

QUITE APPARENT

Doodle, draw, or write the way you saw your parents when you were these ages. Include feelings, shared events, words, fun times, hard experiences, or whatever memories come to mind.

Age 2:

Age 5:

Age 10:

Today:

How do your memories of your parent affect how you feel about him or her today?

How do your parent's memories of you affect how he or she feels about you today?

HERE'S LOOKING AT YOU, KID

Doodle, draw, or write the way you saw your teenager when he or she was these ages. Include feelings, shared events, words, fun times, hard experiences, or whatever memories come to mind.

Birth:

Age 2:

Age 5:

Age 10:

Today:

How do your memories of your teenager affect how you feel about him or her today?

How do your teenager's memories of you affect the way he or she feels about you today?

PARENTS

Complete these sentences about your kids who are in the youth group. Write your answers on your cards—one answer per card. Do not show your answers to anyone.

1. I most worry about...

2. I show I love my teenager by...

3. I get most frustrated when my teenager...

4. I'm really proud of my teenager because...

5. I think my teenager doesn't understand when...

6. My teenager is happiest when...

7. I know I fail my teenager when...

8. I trust my teenager when...

9. I most want my teenager to know that I...

TEENAGERS

Complete these sentences about your parent. Write your answers on your cards—one answer per card. Don't let anyone see your answers.

1. I most worry about...

2. I show I love my parent by...

3. I get most frustrated with my parent when...

4. I'm really proud of my parent because...

5. I think my parent doesn't understand when...

6. My parent is happiest when...

7. I know I fail my parent when...

8. I trust my parent when...

9. I most want my parent to know that I...

MEETING 2: WALK A MILE IN EACH OTHER'S SHOES

Use this meeting to help kids and parents develop empathy for each other's point of view. Give kids and parents a chance to "walk a mile in each other's shoes."

Objectives

Parents and kids will
- describe differences between each other's worlds,
- discover that God has already "walked a mile" in their shoes and understands them,
- put themselves in each other's shoes through role playing, and
- brainstorm five rules for parents and five rules for kids in parent-teenager relationships.

Before the Meeting

Read the meeting, collect supplies, and photocopy the handout. Gather teenage magazines such as Seventeen, Breakaway, and Rolling Stone; scissors; glue; a cassette tape with "space"-sounding music, such as the sound track from *E.T.* or *Star Wars;* a cassette player; magazines adults read, such as Life, Time, Good Housekeeping, and Better Homes and Gardens; a Bible; newsprint; markers; tape; several pairs of shoes; for every four to six group members, two large sheets of poster board and a photocopy of the "Role-Play Situations" handout on page 68.

Think back on your own relationship with your parents during your teenage years. What "cultural" barriers did you face in communicating with them? Think of ways you can help today's kids and parents gain empathy for each other.

The Meeting

1. A FAR OUT PLACE
(up to 15 minutes)

(You'll need poster board, teenage and adult magazines, scissors, and glue.)

Say: **Imagine you have just met someone who fell off**

a space shuttle as an infant and grew up on a planet in outer space. He knows nothing about earth. You have to try to explain your life and customs to him. What differences could you name between his life and yours?

Have kids and parents get into groups of four to six—parents with parents and kids with kids. Hand each group one large sheet of poster board. Give the teenage magazines, scissors, and glue to kids and the adult magazines, scissors, and glue to parents. Tell the groups to make posters of the various aspects of their lives they'd have to explain to the outer-space person. For example, teenage earthlings would have different food, language, houses, clothes, music, and hobbies from an outer-space person.

Play the space music while kids and parents create their posters. When they're finished, turn off the music and say: **Trying to get through to an outer-space person could be tough! You'd have so little in common!**

2. FARTHER OUT
(up to 15 minutes)

(You'll need poster board, teenage and adult magazines, scissors, and glue.)

Have kids, still in their small groups, now try to explain their *parents'* lives to the person from outer space. And have parents try to explain their *kids'* lives to the outer-space person.

Hand each group another large sheet of poster board. Give the magazines adults read to the kids and the teenage magazines to the adults. Tell the kids to make these second posters portray their parents' music, language, food, fashions, and so on. Tell parents to make their posters portray their kids' lives. Turn on the music again while kids and parents work.

When they're finished, turn off the music and display the two sets of posters side by side. Have volunteers explain the posters. Say: **Parents and teenagers can seem like outer-space people to each other! No wonder they have trouble communicating sometimes—they live in two different worlds.**

Briefly discuss particular differences between teenage culture and parent culture; for example, the differences in music. Don't let the discussion become a lengthy rehearsal of stereotypes, however. Not all parents hate the music or clothes that are popular with most kids. And not all kids like them either. The idea is to help kids and parents recognize the differences between their two cultures, not to create differences where none exist.

3. WALK A MILE IN MY SHOES
(up to 20 minutes)

(You'll need newsprint and markers.)

Set up an obstacle course in the meeting room for a "Walk in My Shoes" relay race. Before the meeting, use newsprint and markers to make signs for the different obstacles you plan to have. For example: Make a sign that reads "Relationships Jungle" and tape it up at the obstacle course's starting point. Have a row of people stand there as obstacles. Have "walkers" start out weaving in and out of the people in line. Then have walkers wade through shredded paper called "Frustrations Mire," step over "Hump Day" chairs, crawl under "Embarrassment" tables, jump over a pile of "You Don't Understand Me" books, and finish at "Thank God It's Sunday."

Gather parents into one team and teenagers into another.

Say: **You can't really understand someone else until you've walked a mile in his or her shoes. Now's your chance to do that. Exchange shoes with someone on the other team.**

Have several extra-large pairs of shoes on hand in case you have a different number of parents than teenagers or sizes of shoes that don't match up. After everyone has a "new" pair of shoes on, have the two teams race through the obstacle course.

After the race say: **Jesus, the greatest person ever, came to earth, walked in our shoes, and understood us.** Read aloud John 1:14 and 3:16-17. Ask:

● **What was it like to walk in someone else's shoes?**

● **How did God "walk in our shoes"?**

● **What do you think Jesus felt and experienced as a human that's similar to what we all go through?**

● **What's one way we can be Christlike and put ourselves in someone else's shoes?**

Say: **Teenagers and parents can better understand each other by walking a mile in each other's shoes.**

4. ROLE-PLAYS
(up to 15 minutes)

(You'll need photocopies of the "Role-Play Situations" handout on page 68.)

Use role-plays to help teenagers and parents put themselves in each other's place.

Form groups of four or five, with parents and kids in each group. Give each group a photocopy of the "Role-Play Situations" handout. Have teenagers play the parent's role and parents play the teenager's role. Have the two players try to realistically work things out.

Have groups choose new players when a role-play reaches a conclusion or when players run out of steam.

When groups finish, let them watch the others until all the role-plays are finished. Then get everyone together in a circle and briefly discuss the role-plays. Ask:

● **What did you learn from the role-plays about being a parent? about being a teenager?**

● **How did the teenagers in the role-plays make their parents' job harder? easier?**

● **How did the parents in the role-plays make their teenagers' job harder? easier?**

5. GOLDEN RULES
(up to 15 minutes)

(You'll need a Bible, newsprint, and markers.)

Ask kids and parents to think about what they've observed in the role-plays and in their own relationships. Have a volunteer read aloud Ephesians 6:4 and Hebrews 12:7. Challenge kids and parents to brainstorm "Golden Rules for Parents" in relating to kids; for example, "Listen to your son or daughter before making up your mind about something." Write the ideas on newsprint and have kids and parents rank the top five rules.

Have a volunteer read aloud Proverbs 23:22 and Ephesians 6:2, 3. Challenge kids and parents to brainstorm "Golden Rules for Teenagers" in relating to parents; for example, "Listen to your parents' reasons when they say no to something." Take notes on newsprint and have kids and parents rank the top five.

6. CLOSING
(up to 10 minutes)

(You'll need a sheet of paper and a pen.)

Wrap up the meeting with parents and kids standing in a circle. Encourage kids to speak sentence prayers telling God why they're thankful for their parents and have parents speak sentence prayers telling God why they're thankful for their kids.

Compile and refine the two "Five Golden Rules" lists from the "Golden Rules" activity. Then write the list on a sheet of paper. Make photocopies of the list and give them to parents and kids.

ROLE-PLAY SITUATIONS

● A teenager comes home later than curfew, and the parent is furious.

● A parent has had a rough day at work and comes home to a house pounding with loud rock music.

● A teenager has a disgustingly messy room and refuses to clean it when the parent asks him or her to.

● A parent has just been loudly bickering with his or her spouse and walks into the room where the young person is reading.

● A teenager comes home with grades that are unacceptable to the parent.

MEETING 3: SAYING "I LOVE YOU"

Sometimes it's not easy for parents and kids to express their love to each other. You can help them take the first step.

Use this meeting to help kids and parents learn to say "I love you" to each other. It'll be a gift of God's grace both for kids and their parents.

Objectives

Parents and kids will
- play games that help them express their feelings about family life,
- recognize what they appreciate about each other,
- rate the level of love they share with each other, and
- write letters of affirmation to each other.

Before the Meeting

Read the meeting; photocopy the handouts; gather a Bible, M&M's, 3×5 cards, paper, pencils, twine, tape or tacks, construction paper, clothespins, markers, stamps, and envelopes.

The Meeting

1. LAP LEAP
(up to 15 minutes)
(You'll need chairs arranged in a circle, one for each participant.)

Have kids and parents sit in the circle of chairs.

Say: **Sometimes it's hard for parents to tell their teenagers they love them, and sometimes it's hard for teenagers to tell their parents they love them. The words get stuck. Even though you _do_ love them, it may be hard to show them that love. Today you'll have a chance to think and talk about each other's good points.**

I'm going to read statements that may or may not reflect things you did during this past week. If a statement is true for you, move in the direction I indicate. If it's not true for you, stay seated. If someone is in the seat you're supposed to move to, sit on that person's lap.

Read aloud statements from this list (use as many as time allows):

1. If you said "I love you" to your parent or teenager, move one seat to your right.

2. If you had an argument with your parent or teenager, move two seats to your left.

3. If you fought with your parent or teenager about the bathroom, move one seat to your left.

4. If you helped with the dishes, move three seats to your left.

5. If you yelled at your parent or teenager, move one seat to your right.

6. If you talked about school problems with your parent or teenager, move two seats to your right.

7. If you spent time alone with your parent or teenager and talked, move five seats to your left.

8. If you helped cook a meal, move one seat to your right.

9. If you slammed a door, move three seats to your right.

10. If you lied to your parent or teenager, move seven seats to your right.

11. If you felt your parent or teenager was too busy for you, move three seats to your left.

12. If you argued with your parent or teenager about the telephone, move four seats to your right.

13. If you talked with your parent or teenager about a problem, move four seats to your left.

14. If you cried with your parent or teenager, move eight seats to your left.

15. If you had family devotions together, move five seats to your right.

16. If you had a heated discussion about the music you listen to, move four seats to your right.

After you've said the last lap-leap statement, have parents and teenagers join with their family members to form small groups. Ask:

● **What did you learn about how you relate to your parents or teenagers?**

● **What is your favorite part of your relationship with your parent or teenager? Explain.**

Have the person wearing the most green in each group read aloud Ephesians 6:1-4. Then ask groups:

● **Does this Scripture passage describe what goes on at your home? Why or why not?**

2. BEST VACATION
(up to 15 minutes)

(You'll need a large bag of M&M's, plus a 3×5 card, a sheet of paper, and a pencil for each person.)

Give each person a 3×5 card, a sheet of paper, and a pencil.

Say: **It's important to think of the good times we've shared with our parents or teenagers. On your 3×5 card, write a description of the best vacation or weekend outing you ever had as a family. Don't go into great detail; just write the basics. For example, "We went camping together. It rained. The tents leaked. We got soaked. It was a mess. But we sure had fun." Don't put your name on the card.**

Collect the cards, number them, mix them up, and hand them back to the kids and parents. Make sure no one has his or her own card. Have everyone number their papers up to the number of people participating. Then have kids and parents each read aloud the card they were given. After each card is read, have kids and parents each guess whose vacation it was by secretly writing a name on their paper next to the number of that card. After all the cards are read, ask whose experience each one is. Each correct guess written earns an M&M.

After the game, ask:

● **What was special about all the family adventures we just heard?**

● **What do you still look forward to doing with your parents or kids?**

3. PARENT BRAG-LINE
(up to 15 minutes)

(You'll need a ball of twine, tape or tacks, markers, and plenty of construction paper and clothespins.)

Form groups of no more than four with parents and kids in each group. Have groups discuss these questions. Ask:

● **What makes you feel proud of your parents or teenagers?**

● **What are some big and little things your parents or teenagers do to make you feel special?**

Tape or tack the twine across the room from wall to wall in several places. Place the construction paper, clothespins, and markers on a table in the center of the room.

Say: **On the construction paper, write the ending to this statement: "I'm proud of my mom or dad or son or daughter because . . . " Write as many different responses as you can think of, each on a separate sheet of paper.**

Have kids and parents use clothespins to hang the sheets of paper on the twine. Then have kids and parents walk around and look at the responses. Gather in a circle. Ask:

● **What did you learn about yourself as you started thinking about things your parents or teenagers do that you're proud of?**

● **Why is it sometimes hard to brag about your parents or teenagers?**

4. FAMILY-LOVE REVIEW
(up to 15 minutes)

(For each person you'll need a photocopy of the "Family-Love Review" handout on pages 74 and 75 and a pencil. You'll also need a row of 10 chairs.)

Give each person a pencil and a photocopy of the "Family-Love Review" handout.

Say: **You've had a chance to brag about your parents or teenagers. Now it's time to take a close look at the kind of love you share with each other. The love statements on your "Family-Love Review" handout are taken from 1 Corinthians 13:4-7.**

Read aloud 1 Corinthians 13:4-7.

Say: **In these verses, the Apostle Paul is talking about the meaning of Christian love. Read each statement on your handout and rate yourself—from 1 to 10—on each love quality. Be fair and truthful.**

When all reviews are completed, point out the 10 chairs in a line across the room representing the family-love ratings 1 to 10. Then read aloud each statement in the "Family-Love Review" and have kids and parents each stand by the chair that represents the number they circled on the review. Ask:

● **Why is it hard to show real love to your parents or teenagers?**

● **Where did you rate yourself lowest? highest?**

● **What are some things you can do to raise your lower ratings?**

5. LETTERS TO PARENTS
(up to 10 minutes)

(For each person you'll need a photocopy of the "Love Letter" handout on page 76, a pencil, and a stamped envelope.)

Give each person a "Love Letter" handout and a pencil.

Say: **It's easier to brag about your parents or teen-**

agers when they can't see what you wrote. But they need to know how much you care about them. Complete this love letter to your parents or teenagers. No one but your parents or teenagers will see what you write. Give parents and teenagers a couple of minutes to complete their letters, then ask:

● **How was writing this letter difficult or easy for you?**
● **What effect do you hope this letter will have on the person who receives it?**

Give each person a stamped envelope. Have each person put his or her letter in the envelope, seal the envelope, and address it.

6. GOD'S GRACE
(up to 10 minutes)

Form a circle, then read aloud Romans 5:1-2. Talk about how God's grace is a free gift of love. Then join hands and ask each person to complete this sentence: "Today I learned..." Close with a prayer thanking God for parents and kids.

If it's practical in your area, have kids and parents walk together to the nearest mailbox and mail their letters.

FAMILY-LOVE REVIEW

Read each of the "Love is..." statements. Then rate yourself from 1 to 10 on how much you share that quality of love with your parent or teenager (1=never; 10=always).

1. Love Is Patient

I'm patient with my parent/teenager. I try to see my parent's/teenager's side of issues and understand his or her motives. I'm slow to get angry.

Never   1   2   3   4   5   6   7   8   9   10   Always

2. Love Is Kind

I'm thoughtful and caring toward my parent/teenager. I try to build my parent/teenager up. I appreciate what my parent/teenager does for me and I let him or her know it.

Never   1   2   3   4   5   6   7   8   9   10   Always

3. Love Does Not Envy

I don't get upset when my parent/teenager does something I don't get to do. I don't keep a running score on what my parent/teenager gets to do.

Never   1   2   3   4   5   6   7   8   9   10   Always

4. Love Does Not Boast

I don't try to be the most important person in my family. I don't want excess attention. I work to help my parent/teenager feel important.

Never   1   2   3   4   5   6   7   8   9   10   Always

5. Love Is Not Proud

I don't think I'm better than my parent/teenager. I don't put my parent/teenager down when he or she doesn't measure up to my expectations.

Never   1   2   3   4   5   6   7   8   9   10   Always

continued on next page

FAMILY-LOVE REVIEW (CONTINUED)

6. Love Is Not Rude
I don't mouth off to my parent/teenager. I don't deliberately hurt my parent/teenager with my actions or language.

Never   1   2   3   4   5   6   7   8   9   10   Always

7. Love Is Not Self-Seeking
I don't try to make my parent/teenager conform to my ways of doing things. I don't demand my own way just to make things easier for me.

Never   1   2   3   4   5   6   7   8   9   10   Always

8. Love Is Not Easily Angered
I don't blow up at my parent/teenager when I don't get my way. I don't intentionally irritate my parent/teenager.

Never   1   2   3   4   5   6   7   8   9   10   Always

9. Love Does Not Remember Wrongs
I forgive my parent/teenager. I don't hold grudges against my parent/teenager and I don't make fun of his or her mistakes.

Never   1   2   3   4   5   6   7   8   9   10   Always

10. Love Rejoices in Truth, Not Evil
I don't laugh at my parent's/teenager's failures. I try to encourage my parent/teenager when he or she is facing difficult times.

Never   1   2   3   4   5   6   7   8   9   10   Always

11. Love Does Not Give Up
When I become angry with my parent/teenager, I don't give up on our relationship. I keep trying to work out our disagreements.

Never   1   2   3   4   5   6   7   8   9   10   Always

LOVE LETTER

Dear _____,

Sometimes it's so hard to share my feelings with you. I don't always know what to say. I hope this letter helps.

I love you. I probably don't say that enough.

I really appreciate the way you _____
_____
_____.

I remember a time when you _____
_____,
and I never told you how much that meant to me.

I appreciate how patient you've been about _____
_____
_____.

I never told you how much I admire you for_____
_____
_____.

I wish we could _____
_____
because I think it would help our relationship.

I guess our biggest struggle right now is over _____
_____.
Can we spend time talking about it?

Faith is important to me, but I keep wondering about_____
_____
_____.

I want you to know that I'm glad you're a part of my life. You're the best.

Love,

A RETREAT ON COMMUNICATION FOR PARENTS AND TEENAGERS

Parents and teenagers often fail to effectively communicate simply because they're talking on two different levels. A chasm separates them. Even normally functioning families have difficulty crossing this communication gap. You can help them bridge the gap. Bring teenagers and parents together for a fun, non-threatening day retreat on communication. They'll come away refreshed and affirmed and have the tools they need to understand each other better.

Communication needs to be learned, developed, and practiced. And it has to be practiced by both teenagers and parents. Use this retreat to help teenagers and parents communicate better.

▼ ▼ ▼ ▼ ▼ ▼ ▼ ▼ ▼ ▼ ▼ ▼ ▼ ▼ ▼ ▼ ▼ ▼ ▼

THE RETREAT: LET'S MAKE A DEAL

This one-day getaway will spark family communication and negotiation.

Objectives

Parents and kids will
- improve communication skills,
- learn how to see each family member's point of view,
- discover a pattern for negotiation, and
- learn to set specific rules as a family.

Before the Retreat

Proper preparation of kids, parents, facilities, small group leaders, and yourself is essential for the retreat's success. Use these ideas to ensure a positive day.

1. Inform parents and kids that there will be fun times but also lots of study and interaction time. The retreat isn't primarily a playtime retreat.

2. Find a facility with a meeting room large enough to hold several small groups in the same room.

3. Secure enough small tables (one for each family) and chairs (one for each person) for the "Parent-Teenager Negotiations" activity on page 81.

4. Arrange for two meals and one snack time.

5. Survey your teenagers and their parents to determine conflicts to use as examples in the Bible studies and role-plays. Use the survey on page 84 to give everyone an idea of what you're looking for.

6. Assign adult and teenage leaders to lead the Bible studies in Session 2 (p. 81) and monitor the "Parent-Teenager Negotiations" (p. 81). Give the Bible study leaders the appropriate Bible study handouts.

7. Find songs kids and parents can sing together.

8. Tell participants to each bring a Bible, a notebook, and any sports equipment or table games they'd like to use during the recreation time.

9. Gather construction paper; scissors; markers; straight pins; newsprint; a camera and enough film to take a picture of each family group; a photocopy of either the "Offering Criticism" handout (pp. 86-87) or the "Accepting Criticism" handout (pp. 88-89) for each Bible study leader (one for every four to six people); and a photocopy of the "What is Communication?" handout (p. 85), a pencil, and a 3×5 card for each person.

Retreat Schedule

10:00 a.m.	Beginnings
10:30 a.m.	Session 1: Communication
11:45 a.m.	Lunch
1:00 p.m.	Session 2: Criticism
1:45 p.m.	Snack time
2:00 p.m.	Session 3: Contracts
3:00 p.m.	Recreation and free time
5:00 p.m.	Dinner
6:00 p.m.	Session 4: Celebration
7:00 p.m.	Adjourn

The Retreat Beginnings

1. NAME TAGS
(up to 5 minutes)

Provide construction paper, scissors, markers, and straight pins. Have each person make a name tag that includes
- his or her name and
- a symbol describing his or her family.

Have participants use straight pins to pin on their name tags.

2. SINGING
(up to 10 minutes)

After everyone has made their name tags, gather the group in a circle. Begin with a prayer for God's guidance. Sing favorite songs both kids and parents know.

3. GETTING ACQUAINTED
(up to 15 minutes)

Say: **Today we're going to learn to communicate better with each other. Let's get started by spending a few minutes getting acquainted.**

Form a circle of chairs facing outward. Have parents sit in them. Form another circle of chairs with each chair facing a parent's chair and have kids sit there. Begin by having parent-teenager pairs tell about their name tags. Allow about one minute. Then have kids each move one chair to the right and repeat the process until they arrive back at their original chair.

Session 1: Communication

1. ROLE-PLAYS
(up to 20 minutes)

Ask kids and parents to reverse roles and role play several conflict situations you've developed from the pre-retreat survey. Have kids act like parents and parents act like kids. For example, a teenager wants to stay out past curfew, or a parent is too busy to attend a parents' event with the youth group.

2. "WHAT ARE YOU DOING?"
(up to 20 minutes)

Give everyone a photocopy of the "What is Communication?" handout on page 85 and review the five methods of communication. Ask group members to give examples of each method.

Next, form groups of no more than eight. Have an equal number of parents and kids, all from different families, in each group. Hand out pencils. Have group members list on the back of the handout ways of asking, "What are you doing?"

Encourage group members to use each of the different methods of communicating listed on the "What is Communication?" handout at least once while they're brainstorming ways of asking, "What are you doing?"

3. CONVERSATION LEVELS
(up to 20 minutes)

Have each small group choose two group members to carry on a conversation about the weather or anything else they'd like to talk about. While they talk, have the other group members call out which of the five levels of communication are taking place using their "What is Communication?" handouts. For example, "Nice weather we're having" is level 1—cliché. "Yes, but a low pressure system is moving in" is level 2. "I like sunny days" is level 3. "I hope it doesn't rain because I was planning on going to the park today" is level 4. "I love it when we walk through the park on sunny days holding hands and talking" is level 5.

4. "I" MESSAGES
(up to 15 minutes)

Have groups read the "One communication tool is the 'I' message" section on their "What Is Communication?" handouts.

Ask each person to write two "I" messages on the back of his or her handout. Have them each write a message they'd say to their parent or teenager, then write another message they think their parent or teenager would say to them. These may become the subject of the "Parent-Teenager Negotiations" activity later.

Have volunteers from small groups tell the whole group what they've learned from these communication methods about how to lovingly disagree and reach agreements.

Session 2: Criticism

BIBLE STUDY
(up to 40 minutes)

Form groups of four to six with only parents or only kids in each group. Make sure one of your pre-assigned Bible study leaders is in each group. Give each parent group leader a photocopy of the "Offering Criticism" handout and each teenager group leader a photocopy of the "Accepting Criticism" handout. Have the Bible study leaders follow their handouts to lead their small groups.

Have parents study James 3:1-18 to learn how to give criticism. Have teenagers study portions of 1 Kings 16–18 to learn how to accept criticism. After the Bible study, have someone from each small group report two things the small group members learned.

Session 3: Contracts

1. PARENT-TEENAGER NEGOTIATIONS
(up to 45 minutes)

Explain to participants that contracting between parents and teenagers helps them practice what they've learned. Then have family members follow these steps as they work together to create family contracts.

1. Parents and their kids each form a small family group and sit together around a table. (Provide newsprint and markers for each family group.)

2. Each family group chooses two family conflict situations from the pre-retreat survey or two "I" messages from Session 1 (p. 80) to discuss. For example, use of the family car, leaving dirty dishes in the sink, curfew, music, or choice of clothes.

3. Each person gives his expectations of the situation. For example, the teenager might say, "My friends are important to me, and I need to use the car sometimes to do things with my friends." The parent's expectations might be, "You need to ask before using the car, you need to buy gas for the car, and when you have the car, you need to be home by 11:00 p.m."

4. Discussion continues. Have parents and teenagers use the " 'I' Message" methods from the "What is Communication?"

handout until they each feel understood. Then have the family group discuss how to resolve each conflict situation and volunteer compromises until they reach an agreement.

5. For each situation, when a family group reaches an agreement, they should write it down on newsprint and have all the family members sign it. This is the contract. Celebrate!

6. Continue discussing other conflict situations.

Have adult leaders monitor the negotiations and help family groups that are stuck think of new ways of looking at the conflict situations. Also have someone take pictures of each family group.

2. ROLE-PLAYS
(up to 15 minutes)
Bring everyone back together. Have volunteers role play the same situations role played in Session 1. This time, have parents and kids role play themselves.

Afterward, ask:

● **How was communication different from the first role-plays?**

● **How do you feel when someone is interested in what you have to say? Explain.**

● **Why is it important to listen to your teenager or parent's point of view?**

● **What can you do in the future to resolve a disagreement in your family?**

Session 4: Celebration

1. SINGING
(up to 15 minutes)
Sing group members' favorite songs.

2. LEARNING
(up to 15 minutes)
Form trios. Make sure there's at least one parent and one teenager in each group. Have trios tell each other what they learned about themselves, others, and communications during the retreat.

3. COMMITTING
(up to 15 minutes)
Have people stay in their trios. Give each person a 3×5 card and a pencil. Have each person write what he or she will do to improve family communication. Encourage everyone to explain what he or she wrote to the other trio members.

4. ENCOURAGING
(up to 10 minutes)

Have everyone return to their "Parent-Teenager Negotiations" activity family groups. Have family group members tell each person in their group about a time they admired or felt proud of that person.

Remind parents and kids that they haven't solved all their problems in one day. They'll still have disagreements. They may even break their contracts. But now they have a foundation to build on. They can renew their contracts from the "Parent-Teenager Negotiations" activity or even make new ones.

5. PRAYING
(up to 5 minutes)

Have family groups join hands in small family circles. Ask each person to pray for his or her family. After the family groups finish praying together, pray: **Thank you, God, for our families. Help us understand the other members of our families. Keep us close to them. Amen.**

SURVEY FOR THE RETREAT ON COMMUNICATION

As part of our retreat on communication, we will be role playing disagreements between parents and teenagers. We want this to be as valuable to you as possible so we're trying to gather actual issues that parents and teenagers deal with. Please give us five or so situations that you think parents and teenagers sometimes disagree about. For example, a teenager wants to spend the night at a friend's house but the parents don't know the friend or anything about him or her.

To spark your memory, here are some issues parents and teenagers typically disagree about—curfew, household chores, use of the car, grades, homework, dating, and church involvement. Elaborate on any of these or present other issues.

1.

2.

3.

4.

5.

WHAT IS COMMUNICATION?

PEOPLE COMMUNICATE AT ONE OF FIVE LEVELS.

1. Cliché—"How are you today?" "Fine."

2. Selected facts—"There's a dent in the right front fender of Dad's new car."

3. Idea or judgment—"Blue is a good color to paint my room."

4. All the pertinent facts—"There's a dent in the right front fender of Dad's new car because I hit a fire hydrant."

5. Intimate words—"I love you."

COMMUNICATION IS ACCOMPLISHED IN A VARIETY OF WAYS.

1. Verbally—with words, voice inflection, tone, volume.

2. Bodily—with gestures, posture, expression.

3. Silently—as in "the old silent treatment."

ONE COMMUNICATION TOOL IS THE "I" MESSAGE.

An "I" message expresses personal emotions and facts but doesn't condemn the listener. The formula for an "I" message is "I feel (personal feelings) about (nondestructive behavior) because (how I'm affected personally)." For example, "I feel angry when you won't let me use the car because my friends think I'm a nobody without wheels."

OFFERING CRITICISM
A Bible Study for Parents
JAMES 3

This Bible study will help parents
- learn how criticism affects relationships and
- learn how to be more constructive and less destructive in criticizing their kids.

1. TELL KIDS' CRITICISMS OF THEM.

Have parents each tell what their kids criticize them for. Ask:
- Which criticism bothers you most? Why?

2. BE CAREFUL HOW YOU TALK.

Have a parent read aloud James 3:1-12. Ask:
- What images does James use to illustrate control of the tongue?
- What does each illustration tell about the power of criticism?
- Horse and bit—verse 3
- Poison—verse 8
- Ship, wind, and help—verse 4
- Fountain—verse 11
- Fire—verses 5, 6
- Fruit trees—verse 12
- Animals—verse 7
- Which image best describes your best and worst criticisms of your kids?
- How does criticism affect your relationship with your teenager?

3. BREAK A CYCLE.

Have a parent read aloud James 3:6, 16. Ask:
- What cycle does James outline?
- Where can you most easily break the cycle?

4. TELL AND SHOW.

Read James 3:13. Say: **It's not enough to just *tell* our children what they need to do. We must *show* them.** Then have parents tell areas

continued on next page

OFFERING CRITICISM (CONTINUED)

they're critical of their kids. Write these areas of criticism on newsprint with a marker. Opposite each criticism, write parents' actions that may be hypocritical (ask parents to suggest these hypocritical actions, too). For example:

Criticisms of kids	Parents' hypocritical actions
Listening to rock music	Listening to country-western music
Abusing drugs	Drinking 15 cups of coffee a day
Drinking alcohol	Drinking a cocktail at a party
Being lazy	Failing to attend church
Being dishonest	Cheating on income taxes

5. REMOVE ENVIOUS ATTITUDES.

Have a parent read aloud James 3:14-16. Ask:
● **What do you envy about your kids?**
● **Do you wish you had their free time? their energy? their romance? their age? their opportunities? Explain.**
● **How can this affect your relationship with your kids?**

6. LIVE WISELY.

Have a parent read aloud James 3:17-18. Then have the parents define these words: pure, peace-loving, considerate, submissive, full of mercy, good fruit, impartial, and sincere. Ask:
● **How can each of these characteristics help you give criticism?**

7. DEVELOP GUIDELINES FOR CRITICIZING.

Have parents list guidelines they think are important to follow when criticizing their kids. Then ask parents each to choose one guideline they'll be especially aware of during the coming week in their interaction with their kids.
Close with prayer.

ACCEPTING CRITICISM
A Bible Study for Teenagers
1 KINGS 16-18

This Bible study will help kids
- see that all criticism isn't harmful—some is helpful,
- determine which criticisms they should accept or reject, and
- react properly to criticism.

1. LEGITIMATE CRITICISM.
Ask kids each to make a mental list of things they've been criticized for. Have kids each tell their list to one other person. Ask:
- **Which of these criticisms are legitimate?**
- **Which ones aren't?**
- **Who gives you the most legitimate criticism? the most unjust?**

Say: **Elijah was God's man during the rule of Ahab. But that didn't exempt him from criticism. Everyone is criticized at one time or another. Your job is to discern which criticisms you should listen to and which you should ignore.**

2. THE CRITICISM OF ELIJAH.
First Kings 16-18. Tell kids that when they're criticized, they need to remember these guidelines:
- **Consider the source of the criticism.** Have a volunteer read aloud 1 Kings 18:16-17. Say: **The king of Israel accused Elijah of causing trouble for the nation. But Elijah didn't let that bother him because he knew the source of the criticism.**

Have someone read aloud 1 Kings 16:30-33. Ask:
- **What was the source's problem?**
- **Consider the nature of the criticism.** Have a volunteer read aloud 1 Kings 18:7-15. Say: **The prophet Obadiah had a valid concern. Elijah accepted his criticism and assured the prophet that he'd keep his word. Elijah wasn't offended at Obadiah's criticism but accepted it because it was valid.**
- **Consider the critic's situation.** Have someone read aloud 1 Kings 17:17-18. Say: **Elijah saved this widow from starvation. But the woman turned on him with vengeful criticism. The source was valid—a friend. But the criticism wasn't. Elijah hadn't killed the boy as the widow had complained.** Ask:

continued on next page

● **Why did she say something like that?**
● **Why did she have such bitter criticism?** (Note the circumstances: This woman, a widow, had just lost her son. She probably spoke out of anger and grief.)

3. HOW TO JUDGE CRITICISM FOR YOURSELF.

Give one of these Scriptures to each pair or individual in your group: Matthew 16:21-23 (Peter disputes Jesus), John 18:28-40 (Jesus before Pilate), and 1 Corinthians 5:1-5 (church discipline). Have the pairs or individuals talk or think about the source and nature of the criticism and the critic's situation in the Scripture. Have each pair or individual report to the other kids.

4. UNJUST CRITICISM.

Say: **Unjust criticism is part of life. Remember that you're not responsible for the criticism, but for how you react to it. Jesus was more unjustly criticized than anyone.**

Have a volunteer read aloud 1 Peter 2:22-25. Ask:
● **How did Jesus react to unjust criticism?**
● **How should you react?**

5. REACTION TO CRITICISM.

Have kids choose one legitimate criticism and one unjust criticism from the list they thought of earlier. Ask several kids to tell how they reacted to each criticism. Ask:
● **What could be better reactions? Explain.**
Have volunteers share what they've learned.
Close with prayer.

PART 3

Supporting
PARENTS

KEEPING PARENTS IN TOUCH

After you get parents involved with your youth ministry and their teenagers, you'll want to keep them involved. Keeping parents involved is a matter of keeping in touch with them and keeping them in touch with their teenagers. Keep parents informed about youth-related issues and remind them about important matters concerning your youth ministry. Here are some ways to keep parents informed about activities, youth culture, and youth ministry.

▼ ▼ ▼ ▼ ▼ ▼ ▼ ▼ ▼ ▼ ▼ ▼ ▼ ▼ ▼ ▼ ▼ ▼ ▼ ▼

A Day With the Experts

Schedule a one-day event at which a guest speaker discusses adolescent development. Parents find such sessions helpful in assessing the behavior of their maturing kids and their own reactions to what they observe. Ask the speaker to include pointers on communication skills between parents and teenagers when dealing with issues about spiritual and moral concerns.

Sometimes parents struggle with how to talk to their kids about a specific topic. Plan special evening events with a panel format or individual presentations by respected community or church leaders on "How to Talk to Your Child About Sex...Values...Alcohol...Death"...and so on.

Enthusiasm Breeds Enthusiasm

If you want parents to get excited about your youth ministry, *you* need to be enthusiastic about what's happening. Parents will reflect your commitment and concern. When you talk with parents, smile, laugh, and get them charged up about what the kids are doing. When parents catch your enthusiasm, *their* enthusiasm will have an impact on their kids, other parents, church members, and even on church growth. Families who are considering joining a church often make their choice based on what is offered for young people. Adults are quick to sense from their peers the attitude within the church toward youth ministry. Excited parents provide the best endorsement.

Family Nights

A special evening for the family every now and then is enjoyable for everyone. Activities can take place at the church or some other location in the community such as a school gym or town park. Plan a picnic or recreational activity followed by a time of fellowship. The kids can teach parents (and grandparents, too) the songs they sing whenever the youth group gets together. Kids can also give special reports on their recent trip to the beach or weekend retreat, complete with slides or videotape and other momentos such as banners from each cabin and signs made for the bus.

Helping Parents Plan Ahead

Parents of high school students know that before their son or daughter graduates, decisions must be made about college, a job, or the military. Organize a shelf in the church library or youth office for resources that will help them make those decisions. Include college catalogs, especially of church-related schools. Take group members to college fairs and invite parents to go along. Schedule a "Career Night" and ask church members to talk about their vocations and give the kids (and parents) a chance to ask questions. Invite a college admissions officer to discuss ways to finance a college education.

Hot Spots

Help parents and kids get to know each other better by including a "Hot Spot" column in your church or youth ministry newsletter.

In each newsletter, feature a biographical sketch of one young person and one parent. Group members can volunteer to be reporters and interview each Hot Spot person. Reporters can ask about unusual hobbies, dreams for the future, and one thing the featured people would like to tell their parents (or children).

In addition to being a fun feature, these columns will help kids and parents understand each other better.

Information Nights

When planning a major event or activity with your youth group, providing parents with complete information will help ensure its success. Hold "Information Nights" for parents about upcoming major trips, projects, or experiences. You'll find most parents are appreciative, supportive, and encouraging about their kids' involvement. Give out information and answer questions several weeks or months ahead of time. This helps prevent frustrating surprises or conflicts with family schedules.

Mom and Dad Census

Schedule an annual or biennial visit to homes to meet and talk with parents. When making such a visit, center the conversation on a "census" you're taking. Ask parents questions that provide them an opportunity to tell you any concerns they have about their kids. Then translate these concerns into programs and experiences for the youth group.

Monthly Newsletter

Just as churches send newsletters to keep members informed, a special youth ministry newsletter will keep parents informed about upcoming events and other news that will affect their families, such as dates of special events, program topics, volunteer activities, social gatherings, special projects, and so on. Include information about costs for activities and registration deadlines. Encourage parents to have their kids sign up early. Make the newsletter an attractive piece to post on the refrigerator.

Opening Parents' Eyes

Here's how you can attract parents to a parents' meeting, draw them into your ministry, and open the door to dealing with important parent-teenager issues.

Have kids in your youth ministry each (anonymously) rate their relationship with their parents using "The Kids-on-Parents Quiz" on page 100. Then invite parents to a special meeting to hear the results of your survey. In your invitation, be sure to highlight some of the questions you asked kids.

At the meeting, tell parents the average rating for each question. Then talk about the results. Ask parents how they feel about kids' responses.

After the discussion, give parents each a sheet of paper and a pencil and ask them to write down their answers to the following statements. *(Tell them not to sign their papers.)*

1. The greatest desire I have for my teenager is...
2. The greatest concern I have for my teenager is...
3. The best way the church can minister to my teenager is...

When parents finish, collect the papers. Read aloud their responses to the statements. Parents will soon see that they all face similar problems, and they'll start to feel a sense of community. This should open up communication and build trust between you and them. Then you can tell them how they can help with your group. You should get a good response because you've already drawn them into your ministry.

Parents-Kids Discussion Night

It's natural for parents to get together and talk about their kids, and it's natural for kids to get together and talk about their parents. A real ministry to both provides a setting that encourages dialogue between both groups. Find a skilled counselor in your community who can help facilitate evening programs where kids and parents can discuss any number of youth-related topics. Have kids prepare a set of questions for parents a week in advance. Distribute the questions to parents several days before the meeting. Or, you could have parents write questions for the kids.

Parents Follow-Up Calendar

Sometimes parents want to be involved in your ministry but the timing isn't right. Parents may have other commitments such as church committees, travel for work, projects at home, community commitments, or they may just need a break. Survey parents to find out when their immediate obligations will be fulfilled. Then write parent's names and what aspect of your ministry interests them on your calendar (or the church secretary's calendar) on the dates they will be available. As each date arrives, send a note congratulating the parents on completing whatever task they were working on and telling them how they can get involved in their area of interest. This way you won't miss opportunities to involve interested parents.

Parents' Night

Each September, plan a special evening just for parents. Have everyone who is involved with the youth program, such as pastor, youth leader, and choir director, attend and present the schedule for the upcoming year. This takes careful planning and coordination, but parents welcome knowing well in advance the dates of trips or retreats, when camp is, when the youth choir will sing, when to expect special Sunday school programs, and so on. This is also a great opportunity for youth workers to share their enthusiasm, commitment, and eagerness to work with parents to make youth ministry meaningful.

Parents' Volunteer Survey Sheet

At a parents meeting, or via some other opportunity, provide parents a chance to volunteer to help with your youth ministry. On survey sheets, include tasks such as baking cookies, providing transportation, tutoring, repairing camping equipment, chaperoning dances or trips, leading a small group discussion, and running the movie projector or VCR. All of these tasks give you a chance to work with parents in the areas they're most comfortable with. Use the photocopiable "Parent Survey" on pages 120 and 121.

Reach Out and Touch Someone

The telephone is a simple and time-effective way to keep in touch with parents. Parents welcome calls that don't result in their being asked to do something. Give them a simple, short call to say, "I've been thinking about you today and just wanted you to know." Or you can make the same effective contact with a postcard. It's amazing how many people you can touch if you make one such contact a day!

Soup-and-Sandwich Seminars

Getting parents together for a light lunch is a delightful way to foster fellowship and camaraderie. Invite two or three parents at a time into your home for lunch and conversation. You may have specific ideas to share or just let the conversation flow among friends and listen.

Talk Triggers

In your church bulletin, publish discussion questions for parents and kids to talk about during a meal. Here are some ideas from *Talk Triggers* by Thom and Joani Schultz (available from Group Publishing).

Questions kids could ask parents:
● **What's one of the best memories you have of me as a baby?**
● **What surprised you most about being a parent?**
● **How do you parent differently than your parents did?**
Questions parents could ask kids:
● **Would you marry a non-Christian? Why or why not?**
● **What's one thing you need from me right now?**
● **When you have your own children, how will you raise them differently than you've been raised?**

Tips to Make Your Parents Meetings More Successful

To improve communication with parents, schedule regular parents meetings each quarter or twice a year. A little planning and publicizing will boost attendance and make your parents meetings more effective and enjoyable for all. Before your next meeting, try these pointers:

● Set parents meetings at the beginning of the fall (September), winter (January), and summer (May or early June) seasons.

● FEED your parents. Food is a key to success. In fact, plan a potluck dinner and ask each parent to bring a side dish. (You should provide the main course.)

● Communicate effectively. Send each parent a card or letter about the youth meeting—the date, time, place, what to bring, and when it will end. Also announce the meeting in your church newsletter and from the pulpit. Ask your pastor to show public support and enthusiasm for parental involvement in your ministry.

● The week before the meeting, call *every* parent. Get a verbal commitment from each one to be present. If they can't come, set up an appointment to talk with them later. Take your youth calendar with you when you visit.

● At the meeting, be organized. Start on time. Stop on time.

● Include in your meeting some singing and community building, just as you do in your youth meetings.

● Have on hand samples of curriculum and program materials. Give parents a calendar of upcoming youth meetings and activities.

● Pass out a brochure or flier explaining your church's youth ministry vision, goals, and philosophy.

● Include video or pictures of past youth ministry events. Ask several volunteers to give brief, personal testimonies of how God has touched their lives through the youth group.

● Conduct a question-and-answer time and encourage parents to ask about *anything* that concerns them about your youth ministry, such as discipline, upcoming trips or plans, curriculum, and so on.

● Explain to parents how they can get involved in your ministry through volunteering, praying, providing transportation, chaperoning events, preparing meals or snacks, hosting small groups in their homes, and so on. Ask parents during the meeting to fill out a parent volunteer form. (You might want to use the "Parent Involvement Assessment" form on page 115 or create a form of your own.)

● Close the meeting with an inspirational (but brief) devotional and prayer. Make it an active-learning experience.

Trends and Tips Updates

Growing up today is not the same as growing up a generation or two ago. Kids today are exposed to a broader world than their parents experienced. Give parents a periodic update on what's happening in the youth culture. From professional journals and publications designed for kids, summarize a trend or information on current events in today's youth culture. GROUP Magazine and JR. HIGH MINISTRY Magazine also publish current youth culture trends. Report these in your monthly newsletters to parents. Often these short blurbs can be discussion starters for parents and kids around the dinner table.

Your Open Door

Be available when parents need you. Post your office hours and provide your home and office phone numbers. Assure parents that you're willing to help, whatever the situation. Send parents a business card with your phone number and address and suggest they post it near the phone.

THE KIDS-ON-PARENTS QUIZ

STATEMENTS	NO				YES
1. I know my parents love me.	1	2	3	4	5
2. My parents always treat me fairly.	1	2	3	4	5
3. My parents respect my privacy.	1	2	3	4	5
4. Our family has good and open communication.	1	2	3	4	5
5. I feel free to go to my parents when I have a problem.	1	2	3	4	5
6. My parents contribute to my spiritual growth.	1	2	3	4	5
7. My parents put pressure on me to succeed.	1	2	3	4	5
8. I feel free to discuss sex with my parents.	1	2	3	4	5

AFFIRMING AND ENCOURAGING PARENTS

Parents love to know that their kids' youth minister stands behind them as they work hard to manage a difficult job–parenting. Give your youth group parents a pat on the back for a job well done. Here are some ideas you can use to affirm parents.

▼ ▼ ▼ ▼ ▼ ▼ ▼ ▼ ▼ ▼ ▼ ▼ ▼ ▼ ▼ ▼ ▼ ▼ ▼ ▼

Connecting

Try this idea to affirm kids and parents while helping them communicate.

Create written affirmations about working together or being a part of something. For example, " 'Truly God put all the parts, each one of them, in the body as he wanted them. So then there are many parts, but only one body' (1 Corinthians 12:19, 20). Thanks for doing your part." Then cut the affirmations in half and send one-half of the affirmation to parents and the other half to kids. To get the complete message, kids and parents have to put their halves together! This helps parents and kids see themselves as part of the same team and also helps them realize that you appreciate them.

Courtesy Call

Affirm your youth group parents for a job well done by making a positive "Courtesy Call" at least once every three or four months. A quick phone call to ask how things are going or a short, encouraging affirmation can lift parents' spirits while letting them know you care.

Parents also love hearing praise about their children. During the telephone conversation, give parents a clear example of their teenager's good behavior, such as "I appreciated Tyler when he helped clean up after our lock-in. I didn't even have to ask him to pitch in." Specific examples mean more than general ones like "Tyler is a good kid."

Easy "Parents Night"

A "Parents Night" doesn't require a special agenda. Simply invite parents to attend a regular meeting. When parents attend the youth group meeting, introduce them and encourage them to participate in the activities with their kids. A "Parents Night" lets parents know they're remembered, and it allows them the opportunity to experience a part of their kids' lives.

For-Parents-Only Car Wash

Encourage the kids in your youth ministry to show appreciation for their parents by sponsoring a "For-Parents-Only" car wash.

Schedule a weekend afternoon to hold the car wash. One week before the car wash, have kids create car wash coupons (see example below) and deliver them to their parents. Then on the day of the car wash, have kids wash any car brought in by a parent with a coupon. Don't take any donations, just let this be an opportunity for kids to give something to their parents—no strings attached.

For Parents Only

Dear Parent: Bring this coupon to (place), on (date), at (time), and we'll wash your car ABSOLUTELY FREE. We're doing this for you—no strings attached—as a simple way to say we love you and appreciate you. See you there!

Give Gifts on Special Days

By remembering parents on their special days, you'll let them know they're appreciated. Remind your group members of an upcoming holiday or encourage them to write notes of appreciation on occasion to their parents.

On Mother's Day have group members give moms carnations or balloon bouquets. On Father's Day have group members give fathers Sugar Daddy candy suckers.

Or, declare one Sunday "Parents Day." Have youth group members give anyone who is a parent a smiley sticker or a sticky star for the good job they do.

Hang-in-Theres

Whenever you learn of a family experiencing more than the usual amount of parent-child conflict, try to give a verbal pat on the back to that parent in front of the child.

Inspirational Cards

Sometimes just getting a note with a brief message can give parents a little "pick-me-up." Send postcards with inspirational quotes to parents. Quote uplifting Scriptures such as "Come to me, all of you who are tired and have heavy loads, and I will give you rest" (Matthew 11:28); "Be full of joy in the Lord always. I will say again, be full of joy" (Philippians 4:4); and "Parents who have wise children are glad because of them" (Proverbs 23:24). Or quote a person who inspires you.

A "Love Your Parents" Banquet

Plan a "Love Your Parents" banquet. Valentine's Day is a perfect time to hold the banquet. The format of the banquet is simple: Kids provide the food, service, and entertainment. And parents show up to be fed, served, and entertained.

A parents banquet gives young people and parents a forum to express their love for one another.

"This is the one thing that parents come to who won't come to anything else," says Mark Gold, a youth minister in

Minnesota, after having held 14 "Love Your Parents" banquets. The results have been incredible. Not only have parents enjoyed themselves at the banquets, but many of them have made deeper commitments to Christ.

Tennessee youth minister Heldur Nork, another "Love Your Parents" banquet proponent, says: "Kids and parents don't have much time to work on their relationships with one another. And it's good to have a time when they can both stand back and realize just how much they mean to each other. Kids especially need a time when they're asking what they can do for their parents instead of what their parents can do for them."

Last year, Gold received two touching letters from fathers after his banquet. "One father wrote and told me that as he and his son were walking out of the banquet, his son reached over and hugged him for the first time in his life," says Gold. "The other father heard the words 'I love you' from his son for the first time at last year's banquet."

Good planning is the key to having a "Love Your Parents" banquet that generates such positive responses from parents. Successful banquets include:

● **Personal invitations**—Strongly encourage your kids to ask their parents to the banquet, even if kids suspect they'll be turned down. "Some kids assume their parents won't come, so they don't ask them," says Gold. "But almost every year I run into parents who weren't invited, and they always leave me with the most disappointed looks on their faces."

For some parents, a banquet invitation is like gold. "It's a way to say 'I love you' without coming right out and saying it," says a girl in my church.

Spend part of a group meeting having kids make handmade invitations for their parents. Then collect the invitations and mail them yourself. Keep track of which kids miss the invitation-making meeting so you can have them make an invitation later or make sure their parents are invited. Still encourage kids to invite their parents personally.

● **A quick-and-easy meal**—The food served at the banquet must be easy enough for kids to prepare and serve and tasty enough for parents to enjoy. Lasagna and salad are good choices. Add ice cream and cookies for dessert.

● **Entertainment with a purpose**—Have kids perform a short, gospel-oriented skit or puppet drama during the banquet. (Find skit ideas in *Quick Skits & Discussion Starters* by Chuck Bolte and Paul McCusker or *Fun Group-Involving Skits* by Linda Snyder, Tom Tozer, and Amy Nappa. Both books are available from Group Publishing.) Get as many kids as possible involved in the production.

● **Storytelling**—By far the most attention-getting part of the banquet involves kids' own stories of love and spiritual growth.

● **Words of appreciation**—Have kids introduce their own parents. Then have kids each say something they appreciate about their parents. Tell kids to prepare their words of appreciation before the banquet. Emphasize that only positive things should be said.

● **Notes of appreciation**—Have kids hide notes of appreciation for their parents in the balloons used for decoration. During dessert, have each parent pop a balloon and read the message aloud.

● **Letters to parents**—Have kids write letters to their parents that you can read aloud. Withhold names until the end of each letter. Parents often recognize their child's words early on. One mother burst into tears when she heard her daughter's words, "Can we start over?"

● **Kids' ideas**—Let your kids come up with their own ideas for affirming parents. This can give kids even more ownership for the banquet and add personal touches that make the banquet more intimate and special.

A "Love Your Parents" banquet might well transform some of the families in your church.

Parent Speakers

The parents of youth group members are a wonderful resource with varied skills, careers, and life experiences. A youth group can both honor them and benefit from their knowledge by inviting them to share.

The Personal Touch

Everyone likes to be remembered and appreciated. Write thank-you notes whenever a parent lends a helping hand. Send a note when a parent has a special occasion, a sad time, or an accomplishment, such as a wedding anniversary, birthday, marriage, death in the family, a new job or promotion, joining a church committee, election to a board, or receives community honors.

Presenting...Parent Awards!

Have kids design awards for their parents by writing one of these verses on each award: "Children, obey your parents as the Lord wants, because this is the right thing to do" (Ephesians 6:1), or "The father of a good child is very happy...Make your father and mother happy; give your mother a reason to be glad" (Proverbs 23:24-25). Have kids personalize the awards by also writing on them the things they appreciate most about their parents. During church announcements, have youth group members present their parents with the handmade awards. Call parents forward and have kids pin or tape the awards on them. Afterward, challenge church members whose parents are alive to call or write them and thank them for all they've done.

Striking the Right Notes

Parents welcome notes about their children. Write notes to parents about the qualities you appreciate in their kids. Also, a simple postcard praising their child's achievement at school, part in the school play, or solo at a community concert lets parents know you care. This will open the door to closer contact with parents when you see them at church.

Take a Parent to Lunch

Most people eat lunch, it's just a question of where and when. Arrange a lunch-time chat with a parent to let them know you've been thinking of them. This also gives you time to visit without being surrounded by kids.

Thanks for Your Kids

On youth group members' birthdays send their parents a card as well as the kids. Thank the parents for accepting the responsibility to bring the child into their home and care for him or her. If they are the biological parents, thank them for bringing the child into the world. Be sensitive to how they became parents of the child—whether through birth, adoption, or remarriage.

Visit Parents at Their Place of Employment

The overwhelming majority of parents work. Arrange your schedule so you can drop by their work (if appropriate) just to say hello. Also, if you are in need of a service such as repair work, try to discover if one of the kids' parents is employed in that field.

HANDLING CONFLICT WITH PARENTS

Building positive relationships with parents reduces your chances for conflict with them. In spite of our best efforts, though, conflict does arise. Since parents are an essential part of your youth group kids' lives, it's important to face conflicts and reconcile relationships as much as possible.

Use these guidelines to work through conflict and support unsupportive parents.

▼ ▼ ▼ ▼ ▼ ▼ ▼ ▼ ▼ ▼ ▼ ▼ ▼ ▼ ▼ ▼ ▼ ▼

Face the Conflict

You may be uncomfortable with some aspect of a parent's involvement, a parent may confront you, or you may hear from someone else that a parent is upset with you. Speak directly to the parent. Ask to talk and pray with the parent about the situation. If you are unable to talk right away, set up an appointment to talk as soon as possible. Don't cause the parent to "lose face" in front of kids or other parents by confronting him or her at church or when others are around.

Listen

We communicate empathy, understanding, worth, and concern when we listen seriously and attentively to one another. Scripture says, "Let everyone be quick to listen, slow to speak, slow to anger" (James 1:19). Don't try to resolve every conflict "on the spot." A parent may need to vent hostility before constructive dialogue can occur. Don't interrupt. You'll get your chance.

You can understand the parent better and show you value the parent and his or her concern by asking questions and paraphrasing what the parent says. Ask questions to clarify, not intimidate. Paraphrasing back the parent's statements and reflecting back the parent's feelings gives him or her a chance to clarify anything you've misunderstood.

Avoid Defensiveness

Don't get defensive or put down parents you disagree with—either to their faces or behind their backs. Instead try to understand where they're coming from and clarify for them what they don't understand.

Take Responsibility

Admit the truth about what may be wrong. Calmly and lovingly speak the truth about what parents might have misunderstood. For example, a parent might confront you about how you corrected his or her teenager at a youth meeting. Be honest. Were you too rough on the teenager? Did you embarrass the teenager in front of his or her friends?

Do you need to talk to the parent about taking steps to improve the teenager's behavior? If disrupting meetings has become a habit, calmly and lovingly talk with the teenager and his or her parent. Explain how valuable the teenager is to the youth group and discuss ways you can work with them to make your meetings more successful for you and the teenager.

Ask for Forgiveness

Youth ministers do make mistakes. All sides bear some responsibility for most conflicts. Face your weaknesses honestly and openly. Parents will develop deep respect for you when you admit your own vulnerability. Ask for forgiveness, then state how the situation will be handled in the future. For example, if you reacted harshly to a teenager, apologize to the parent and the teenager. Promise that you'll try to be more sensitive in the future.

Agree to Disagree

Sometimes you may not be able to agree with parents because they disagree with a basic church doctrine or policy. Remember, people can work together even if they disagree.

Resolve Conflict Immediately

The Bible tells us not to let the sun set on anger (Ephesians 4:26). Even if we can't agree, as people we need to be reconciled. At times, conflicts may need to go before the pastor or a committee to get resolved. Use these resources to constructively and immediately relieve tension, not as a threat. If you meet with the pastor or committee, make sure that the parent's side is as clearly presented as your own.

Recognize That Conflict Can Be Good

The bad news is that conflict can sometimes strain relationships and cause hurt feelings. The good news is that every conflict with parents can be a learning, growing experience. Learn to view problems with parents as possibilities for deepening your relationships with them and for experiencing God's grace.

Evaluate the Criticisms

Take the time, no matter how painful the process, to discover the root cause of parents' dissatisfaction. Ask questions and don't discount answers. If parents raise a specific concern or problem, think about it. Are they justified? If so, what changes could be made in your ministry? How will you make those changes?

It's dangerous to set your ministry approach in stone. Show parents their concerns are important to you by listening, evaluating, and making adjustments when necessary. But don't compromise your spiritual convictions in the process.

Avoid the Temptation to Play Favorites

So a parent hasn't treated you fairly? In fact, maybe he or she has been downright nasty. Watch out! You may consciously or unconsciously begin to invest less time and energy in that person's kids. We're tempted to favor kids of supportive parents. Not only is that wrong, but kids notice what's going on. Sometimes, kids from families that don't support you may be living in a negative home environment and actually need *more* concentrated care.

Encourage Supportive Parents to Reach Out to Unsupportive Parents

Unsupportive parents will often open up when supportive parents ask them to get involved. Supportive parents' enthusiasm may be just the spark an unsupportive parent needs.

Pray

Remember that God can change hearts and give insight and wisdom. Pray diligently for any unhealthy relationships with parents that you may have in your group. When necessary, change your approach. Sometimes the parents come around; other times the circumstances change.

Don't Lose Sleep

Walt Mueller, author and youth minister, says, "Once I responded to a parent's criticisms by planning an event just the way she wanted it. A few hours after the event, she called to tell me I'd failed again."

Sometimes the problem is beyond your control. Even when you work hard at building support from parents in your church, every church has parents who enjoy being critical. The solution? Just keep up the good work!

PART 4

FAST FORMS

Parent Involvement Assessment

Recognizing a need is the starting place for meeting that need. Photocopy the "Parent Involvement Assessment" handout on page 115 and have your youth ministry team members (including you) and parents each fill one out. Discover how much parents are (or aren't) involved in your program.

Then brainstorm with parents ideas for improving parent involvement. Begin improving parent involvement in the areas that received the lowest scores.

Remember, this tool is to help you evaluate and improve parents' involvement in your ministry. Don't use the results to fuel blame or criticism.

PARENT INVOLVEMENT ASSESSMENT

How do you think our youth ministry rates with parent involvement? Mark a score from 1 (Boo!) to 10 (Yea!) for each area below.

_____1. Parents volunteer to help with activities.

_____2. Parents support with adequate funding.

_____3. Parents serve on youth ministry committees.

_____4. Parents help with snack suppers or meals.

_____5. Parents chaperone and drive young people to activities.

_____6. Parents tell others in our community about our church's youth ministry.

_____7. Parents read information we send them about youth activities.

_____8. Parents support youth ministry staff and sponsors.

_____9. Parents help with fund-raisers.

_____10. Parents pray for and spiritually reinforce their kids' and other church kids' Christian faith.

Time, Talent, and Interest Form

The "Time, Talent, and Interest Form" on pages 117 and 118 offers a quick and easy way to identify parents' gifts. It may also be used to identify areas of need within your youth group and may encourage parents to offer their skills and services for various activities.

TIME, TALENT, AND INTEREST FORM

The youth program in our church needs your help. Please check those areas below where you would be willing and able to serve. Thank you!

Advertising/Publicity

____ Prepare mailings

____ Prepare bulletin boards

____ Prepare posters

____ Prepare newsletters

____ Other _____

Worship/Celebration

____ Drama (direct, write, design sets or costumes, help with makeup, help with special events like the Christmas program or the Easter Sunrise service)

____ Clown ministry

____ Puppet ministry

____ Prepare banners

____ Other _____

Education

____ Lead Bible study

____ Teach a class (church membership, confirmation, Sunday school, etc.)

____ Plan program (check out missions projects, set up parent/youth activities)

____ Other _____

Service

____ Visit members (shut-in, hospital, inactive, new)

____ Homework hot line (subjects, grade levels)

____ Drive a car

____ Drive a bus

____ Teach how-to skills for (_____)

____ Library (checkout/in, review books)

____ Teach time management

____ Phone (call for polls, activities, other)

____ Share your hobby

____ Host activity at your home

____ Talent search (help others identify their skills)

____ Kitchen help (serve, clean up)

____ Prepare food

____ Provide refreshments

____ Coach a sports team (softball, soccer, basketball, tennis, other)

____ Listen to people

____ Other _____

____ Other _____

continued on next page

TIME, TALENT, AND INTEREST FORM
(CONTINUED)

Activities

____ Retreats (junior high, high school)

____ Lock-in

____ Ski trip

____ Fund-raisers

____ Service projects

____ Workcamp

____ Mission trip

____ Cantata

____ Other_____

Audio-Visual

____ Run machines

____ Teach how to use equipment

____ Use equipment to create programs

____ Sound system

____ Slide projector

____ Opaque projector

____ Video camera

____ Take pictures

____ Other_____

Music

____ Choir (sing, direct, other)

____ Play an instrument (piano, guitar, etc.)

____ Accompany others

____ Hand bells (play, teach direct)

____ Other_____

Name _____ Phone number _____

Address _____ Date _____

Parent Survey

The "Parent Survey" on pages 120 and 121 offers an easy way to ask for feedback from parents and determine how they might be interested in being involved. Since youth programs vary considerably, use the following instrument as a guide for developing your own survey.

Two-way communication is important for successfully involving parents in your program. Share the results of this survey with both the parents and the kids in your group. Use the results to open the doors of communication between parents, kids, and the church. Provide opportunities to answer the questions and needs of parents. Involve those parents who indicate a desire to help or serve. When you ask parents for their input and then offer opportunities for them to get involved, they are much more inclined to support your efforts and their kids' involvement.

PARENT SURVEY
How Can We Help You?

The youth group at our church is your youth group, too. We are interested in your input and assistance to help make this the best youth group possible. Please take a few moments to complete the following survey.

Name _____ Phone number _____

Address _____ Date _____

How can the youth program serve the needs of your kids?

How can the youth group leader(s) help support your needs as a parent?

What expectations do you have of the youth leader(s) and the youth program?

What suggestions do you have?

What days and times for youth meetings and events are most convenient for your family?

continued on next page

PARENT SURVEY
(CONTINUED)
How Can You Help Us?

Would you be willing to help in one or more of the following areas?
(Indicate yes or no and fill in the best day or time.)

Provide refreshments for a meeting?   Yes   No
Best Time/Day _____

Host a meeting at your home?   Yes   No
Best Time/Day _____

Be a driver for an event?   Yes   No
Best Time/Day _____
If yes, are you licensed to drive the
church van or bus? _____

Be a special speaker for a meeting?   Yes   No
Best Time/Day _____

Assist in planning a meeting?   Yes   No
Best Time/Day _____

Be a volunteer for a one-time event?   Yes   No
Best Time/Day _____

Serve on the youth advisory council?   Yes   No
Best Time/Day _____
(One meeting a month)

Other ways you would like to help: _____

_____

_____

What questions or concerns do *you* have about the youth program?
(Please use the back of this page.)

Parent Information Form and Parent Commitment Letter

It's helpful to seek as much information as possible about youth group members' parents or guardians. This knowledge will help you meet the needs of your teenagers through relationships and programming.

Two settings offer excellent opportunities for obtaining this information: a parents' meeting early each fall or individual interviews with parents during a visit to their home. Mailing this form to parents and expecting them to return it is the least effective way to obtain this information since response would be minimal.

Assure parents that you will keep the "Parent Information Form" on page 123 confidential. That way parents won't feel that other church programs will recruit them based on the information on this form.

Update your information forms annually. If possible, attach a picture of the family to your form. Fill out forms on non-member families. These are excellent resources for outreach and evangelism.

The "Parent Commitment Letter" on page 124 should be signed at the end of each parents' meeting or after a home visit by the youth minister. Listen to parents who hesitate or refuse to sign this letter. They may have deep concerns or needs that warrant pastoral care.

PARENT INFORMATION FORM

Young person's name (Last name first) _____

Mother's name _____

Father's name _____

Guardian (If applicable) _____

Other siblings and ages _____

_____

Street address _____

City _____ Zip _____ Phone _____

Mother's occupation _____

Place of employment _____ Phone _____

Father's occupation _____

Place of employment _____ Phone _____

Mother's hobbies, interests, sports _____

_____

Father's hobbies, interests, sports _____

_____

Marital status   ___Married   ___Separated
                    ___Divorced   ___Widowed

Address and phone of noncustodial parent (If applicable) _____

_____

Comments _____

_____

continued on next page

PARENT INFORMATION FORM
(CONTINUED)

Use the initials of each parent to mark areas of interest or to indicate where he or she is willing to volunteer:

___ Snack supper   ___ Work with evening fellowship

___ Provide transportation   ___ Work with youth choir

___ Youth librarian   ___ Youth council

___ Sponsor at youth events   ___ Help with youth fund raising

___ Teach   ___ Host meetings

___ Visit families with prospective new youth

___ Assist young people with service projects

___ Other (_____)

List any special skills or talents (such as drama, clown ministry, puppets, photography, carpentry, cooking, mechanics, and so on) that either parent might be willing to share with our young people: _____

_____

What do you think parents expect the church's youth ministry to do for their children? _____

_____

What do you think parents need from the church's youth ministry?

_____

_____

PARENT COMMITMENT LETT

Dear Parent(s) or Guardian(s):

Today, _____, you attended the parents' meeting or visited with the
                (date)
youth minister about the following items:

- the youth calendar for _____ through _____;
                          (month)   (month)
- the volunteer tasks that are needed from parents during this time
  period;
- the code of conduct for young people in our youth programs;
- program materials and study topics for youth meetings in our church;
- curriculum taught in our Sunday school;
- plans for youth lock-ins, trips, and retreats, including costs and
  details; plus
- the long-range goals and objectives for our youth ministry program.

If you approve of these plans and programs, please indicate your support by doing the following:

- encourage your teenager to participate;
- bring your young person to youth activities, if necessary;
- volunteer for tasks you are willing to undertake;
- affirm the importance of youth ministry to other adults within the
  congregation;
- support funding for youth ministry by giving to the church budget;
  and
- pray for all our young people, plus the volunteers and church staff
  who work with them.

If you are willing to make this commitment, please sign this letter on
the lines below.

_____

Mother (or Guardian)

_____

Father (or Guardian)

Appreciation Letter

Thank-yous are appropriate for parents who have fixed a snack for refreshments, helped with transportation, been guest speakers or resource people for programs, raised money for an event or provided scholarships, provided free materials or services to the youth group, chaperoned an activity, taught a youth class or sponsored the youth group, hosted a youth activity, or stood up as advocates for youth ministry in church committees or board meetings. Thank-yous are appropriate for any parent who has been involved in any way.

To personalize your thank-you, add a handwritten note mentioning the specific contribution you're grateful for. And remember, you can never say thanks too much. Send appreciation letters often.

APPRECIATION LETTER

Date_____

Dear _____,

I want you to know how much the youth group and I appreciate your help with _____.
Your service greatly supports our congregation's youth ministry.

Too often we forget to say thank-you for the many ways you have demonstrated your love and caring for the young people in our congregation. For all your past support and your future assistance, we give thanks to God.

Yours in ministry with youth,